Aubrey Beardsley, Vincent Brown

My brother

Aubrey Beardsley, Vincent Brown

My brother

ISBN/EAN: 9783337141721

Printed in Europe, USA, Canada, Australia, Japan

Cover: Foto ©Andreas Hilbeck / pixelio.de

More available books at **www.hansebooks.com**

MY
BROTHER

BY
VINCENT BROWN

❦

LONDON
JOHN LANE
THE BODLEY HEAD
CHICAGO
RAND McNALLY & CO.
1896

Copyrighted in the United States
All rights reserved

MY BROTHER

I

"No, no; we must stick to the peacocks," Lord Lusson said. "If they are a bit untidy, they make up for it by completing the picture. See that one on the terrace there, against the red creepers—the genius of pride and the genius of colour. They realise life: the old place wouldn't look the same without the peacocks. And my mother was very fond of them."

The young man, in a pleasant social temper, strolled on the grass, a cigarette between his fingers, a collie at his heels. The gardener fell silent, having said his ill word for the peacocks. Swallows made magic lines in the sunny air: on a lake, set amid trees and undergrowths, swans idled perfectly; the laughter of children came from the home park, where the turkey-cocks, in excess of vanity, were making themselves ridiculous. Lord Lusson, catching sight of an uncouth figure standing in a gap in an old wall (that was embroidered with beautiful things), made a somewhat irritable gesture.

"Who is that man, Reid? I have seen him about the place several times of late. I came upon him again yesterday in the rhododendron walk in the Little Wood; that seems to be his favourite loafing-ground. Who is he?"

"It's the Prophet, my lord."

The figure disappeared.

"Is he a tramp?"

"Not by profession, my lord, though his manner of life comes near to the same thing. He does odd jobs for the farmers and in the small gentry's gardens when he's able. But he has a damaged spine, or something, and that keeps him from putting in a decent man's work."

"He looks deformed. He is always alone when I see him."

"—— unless when there's children with him," said Reid.

" Is he married ? "

The gardener (having a sense of humour) smiled. " No, my lord, he's not got a wife yet. Some women are not over particular, but there's hardly a woman in Occlesby who'd not draw the line at the Prophet."

" Has he a bad character then ? "

" I'd not say that of him, my lord. It's not his character, but his feeble body and spirit that's the obstacle. He's such a poor wreck of a creature."

" Oh, quite so. Why is he called the Prophet ? "

" The name grew up with him; except for his queer religious opinions, I can't say why. He's not so old as he looks, because of his beard, and those ancient eyes of his, and the way he hobbles about on his big blackthorn. I remember him a little lad, when nobody could make head or tail of him ; his dullness was beyond words. His mother's dead, and there's always been a mystery who his father was. He lives alone, and has done these many years, in a hut in a dell off the Alveton Road. He made it himself, helped by some —Willie May, mostly—that had regard for his feckless loneliness. He has gipsies for neighbours generally, unless when the children go to see him. But nobody would meddle with the Prophet."

"I suppose he lives by poaching?"

The gardener shook his head.

"I doubt if he has the heart for a poacher, my lord."

"But what is his name?"

"Paul Penfold."

"Quite so." Lord Lusson moved up the steps on to the terrace. "I shall be leaving in a day or two, Reid," he said, turning, "and of course you will see that everything goes on all right here."

"Yes, my lord."

"There has been a little too much licence of late; people seem to imagine that this place is kept up for their convenience. I fancy my mother spoilt them—but one likes to feel sure of being alone sometimes. It is time at least to put a stop to the abuse of the

Little Wood; the rhododendron walk has been turned into a public thoroughfare. It is nothing of the kind, and I shall have a notice-board put up. Oh," he added, "you might tell Anscombe to have these white bantams fastened up; they scratch and cackle all day long, and keep coming into the house. I found a couple roosting in the hall last night, and there was a fine shindy when I tried to catch them."

Reid said again, "Yes, my lord," and went on to the gardens. Lord Lusson sat on an old bench, among honeysuckle, and looked at the peacocks through cigarette smoke; the collie rested its muzzle on his knee. The peacocks minced down a grassy slope to the water, and the white bantams made for the home-park, bent on fare more satisfying than grubs. But Lord Lusson sat with his thoughts till the declining of the day.

II

Now Paul, being of a peaceable spirit, made no fuss of the matter, when, trudging homeward in the mid-afternoon (having neatly trimmed the rectory lawn), he was hauled by Andrew Isted into the Lusson Arms, and bidden drink a glass of ale. He offered thanks for the courtesy, and set the glass on the bar counter, assuring the village gossips that ale was a liquor that agreed not with the temper of his stomach.

"Then it should," said the innkeeper, "or your stomach's not proper English."

"You always was a horrible unpractical chap, Prophet," Andrew Isted said. "And what's to come of you, now the Little Wood's been closed? No more moony rambles there, Prophet. My lord's put up a notice, new painted on a white painted board, to keep out all you dreamin wanderers and tramps.

He's in a mighty fret about it, they say."

"Thank God," said a big man, "I never go by the rhododendron path myself, havin a trap."

"Everybody's not got traps," said Paul, "and if they had, some might think of them that hadn't." Andrew Isted laughed. "It's been in livin memory the short cut to Danbridge," Paul added, "and it's wrong, I do think, for Lord Lusson to close it. I'd not like, if I was a great high lord, to have my name stained with oppression of the poor. If it was in Danbridge, where there's them that have a jealousy for the rights of common folk, he'd not dare to do it."

"Look you now," said Woolven the saddler, "that's downright rampant Radical doctrine, and I'm not sure if it's not traitorous to the law of the Constitution."

"Oh, but the Prophet never knows what he says five minutes at a time," the innkeeper growled. "He's muddled up here in his intellect, like most that scorns good old English ale."

"There's nothing like ale for settlin a man's political opinions," said the big man.

"Here's to their settlement," laughed Andrew Isted.

"I'll tell you what, Prophet," said Woolven the saddler, "if you wasn't a kind of Christian in your own style, you'd have been a most dreadful depraved Radical. I'm not sure," gasped the saddler, "whether you'd not have given your mind even to Socialism, or that worse principle where they teach infernal machines. You're just of that stamp, Prophet, very like the colour of them that's unbalanced in mind and shaky in fortunes. I maintain, which I always have done, and always will, whatever anybody may say, that the Tory doctrine is the only doctrine that falls in line with natur."

"My sentiments to a T," said the innkeeper.

"Mine," said the big man, "if they was stronger expressed."

"Well, gentlemen," said Paul, going out at the door, "I'll leave you to your agreements, and walk up and see my lord's notice with my own eyes, more particular as the scent of ale on a fine day makes me feel rather giddy."

"Now I call that an abominable insult," said the innkeeper.

"It shows the weakness of his head," said the big man.

"I've never been decided whether he's more a knave or a fool," said the saddler. "There's points in his credit. The women takes to him."

"H'm," said Andrew Isted.

"Oh, he's harmless enough," cried the saddler. "I've never heard of him what I've heard of you, Andrew. He's over low in his health, with that broke back of his, to do mischief either among the fair or in the commonwealth, though I've a shrewd notion the bee in his bonnet is just the sort that wants to do it."

Paul sauntered up the hillside leisurely to the Little Wood. A little child came to him, and he took its hand, and prattled to it with a marvellous gentleness and simplicity. Paul held the secret that opened children's hearts. On the grassy sunlit road outside the gate of the rhododendron path, a group of little ones were lying down watching something intently. Paul moved up to them cautiously, and saw that it was a baby toad. "It's overcome by the sun," said he, and picking it up, put it in the ditch. "They don't like much sun, the toads," said Paul. The children gathered round him: one wee lassie, with a head like the head of the child in Titian's "Bacchus and Ariadne," wormed her hand up his sleeve till it came to his elbow.

"Letty Tomsett," said Paul, "you're spyin out how bony I've grown."

"I feels your funny bone," said Letty.

"Well, then, leave it alone," said Paul. "You'll want to know next what I've had for my dinner."

"What?" said Letty.

"I donno if I'll tell you, for your inquisitiveness. Oh, my, and here's that impident Teddy Barton up my other sleeve. I never did see sich children for pullin a man in pieces. I'm not a Punch and Judy show like you saw in your Sunday school treat."

He sat down on the grass, and the children scrambled over him. One little girl got behind him, put her arms round his neck, and began to blow in his ear. Another, sitting on his foot, was doubled up with laughter.

"What for do you always laugh so, Susan Peacey, whenever you see me?" Paul asked. "One would think you was frightened of me."

"I'm not frightened," Susan Peacey said.

"Then what for do you laugh?"

"You're such a funny man."

"Me a funny man?" said Paul, opening wide his eyes in counterfeit amazement: whereat all the children laughed. "Dearie me. There now, hear that wild language; why, I thought I was the most solemn, long-faced, terrible, grim man, like the ogre in the fairy tale—Oock!" He made a fearsome snap with his mouth. The children screamed with laughter.

"Do it again," one said; and they all cried, "Do it again; do it again, Paul!"

"No; I'll not do it again, for fear you

might think of me after with that ugly face. I'll tell you a nice story, and that'll be ever so much better than being a ogre."

"Jack the Giant Killer!" said Teddy Barton.

"No; I'm not feelin like Jack to-day," said Paul. "I'd not be able to enter on the narrative with spirit."

"The old woman that lived in a shoe," cried Susan Peacey.

"Well, I might deal with the old woman in a finer sincerity. But you've heard it before, and I donno if it's improvin to the mind to be constant goin over the same theme, when there's a doubt whether it's founded on fact. I'll give you a Scripture story instead, and you must remember it's true, and not the kind of story for gigglin purposes."

So he told them of Joseph and his brethren; and when he was done, "I wonder why our mothers don't make coats like that now," Teddy Barton said.

"It's because to keep you children from bein vain, no doubt," said Paul, "which is a sad temptation, and one that opens the door to almost every wrong."

A little boy made a grab at something in the air.

"Don't touch it," said Paul; "it's a spider workin at its web. Just look how he's doin it. Ssh—stop your breath, Teddy. Wonderful, wonderful. You must never kill a spider, children; it's bad luck to."

"But they're cruel themselves, and kill flies and things," Teddy protested; "so, if you kill them, it only pays them out."

"That's true, so far," said Paul, "but it's no argyment. We may wonder, as I offen do, what the insects consider of our care of the young birds in the spring, that's waitin for a chance to wolf them up; but it's not for us to go behind sich mysteries. Everything is in a perfect law, if we could but see it."

"Why can't we?" Teddy asked.

"How should I know?" said Paul. "God made it, and never took none of us into His confidence when He done it. But we do know it couldn't have been better done, not if all the men and women and children in the world — includin that conceited big man Teddy Barton — had tried their hands at it."

Paul had forgotten for the time the purpose of his walk to the Little Wood. But when the children were gone, he went close to the gate, and read the warning to trespassers that was nailed to a tree. He stood regarding it with a preoccupied air: yet with no harsh feeling against the young man who had had it put up there. And presently, as he made his way westward along by the wood, he searched mentally the Book of the Prophet Ezekiel (for whose writings Paul had a strong partiality) for words concerning trespassers of another kind. He could not recall anything from Ezekiel which just suited the case: so his mind went burrowing far and near in the Scriptures. But the words somehow continued to baffle him. "They're on my tongue," he said to himself: "but I can't bring them in their true shape."

He stopped to look at a blue butterfly on meadowsweet, and fell in a muse. "The wise sad men," he thought, "dream of the golden days, while the butterflies and the children live in them." He sighed. "It makes a world of difference, and makes us think that innocence is life, and knowledge pain."

He went on. "I do feel," he said to himself, "I'd like a nice cup of tea." He stopped again, looking towards the village. "Ay; I'll go and ask Mrs May if she'll give me a cup." He came off the road, and made his way across the hillside back to the village.

In half-an-hour Paul (being slow of gait) reached Mrs May's cottage. It stood off a by-path, in a garden, and was a very humble dwelling. There were two tiny windows and a door in front, and on opening the door you were at once in the living-room. Most of the Occlesby cottages were after this pattern; in some, five or six children slept in one bed, feet to feet. Never an autumn passed but young men and young women died of consumption. Others went forth, to Danbridge and elsewhere, to seek their fortune, and came home to die. The rents were low; and nobody seemed to think that anybody was to blame.

Paul had begun again to search the Scriptures in his head, but he gave this up on arriving at Mrs May's cottage. "I'll look in the concordance when I get home," he said to himself. He tapped at the door, opened it without being bidden, and entered.

III

HE shut the door behind him, very softly; and having placed his blackthorn in a corner, put his hat on the floor beside it, and then: "Good day, Mrs May," said he. The elderly woman seated on a stool by the fire looked round at him with troubled eyes, but made him no answer. Some one was weeping in the bedroom.

"Mrs May——"

"Paul," she said, "I'm glad you've come." She seemed not to wish to let him see her face.

The bedroom door was shut, and the weeping was less violent after Paul entered the living-room. There were now low sobs, as though a person were lying with face hid in bedclothes. Paul stood silent awhile.

"Mrs May——"

"I'm glad you've come, Paul," she said again. "Won't you sit down, Paul."

The invitation lacked urgency; but Paul knew that he was welcome. This had been to him a kind of second home; Mrs May had dressed his mother for burial. He sighed as he took the chair opposite to her on the hearth. Mrs May began to put bits of wood on the fire. She was a worn, thin, weary woman; as she leaned towards the fire Paul's gaze rested on her shoulders, and he saw how the blades came out in sharp angular outline under the small black shawl she was wearing. In her hands and wrists, when he looked at them, he read a pathos still more acute. She stooped to blow the fire, and at that moment Paul had a vision of a Figure kneeling in a garden by the Syrian shore. The weeping in the next room gave intensity to his inward sight, a poignant note to his sympathy.

"You say you're glad I've come, Mrs May."

"Yes, Paul. It's about Lizzie."

Mrs May turned to him: hers was a long, serious, sad face, full of the dignity of reticent suffering: a face on which one might expect to see a smile of gratitude when at last its tired eyes should look on death.

"Lizzie," Paul said. "About Lizzie. What's she cryin for, Mrs May?"

"Oh, Paul, can't you guess?" And the mother looked into his eyes, and Paul, understanding, sat in a silence that was like paralysis of mental and physical faculties. Lizzie's mother bowed her head before him, and there was weeping in both rooms now.

Paul was so moved with compassion that he could see only the blurred outline of a woman for his tears. He glanced at the inner door, then bent his head down to Mrs May and whispered—

"Lord Lusson?"

"Yes, Paul. So she says——"

"It's true!" Paul said, raising his voice. It's been in my mind, Mrs May, that wickedness was bein done. He had the look of one of the destroyers—not a cruel man, deliberate-like, mebbe, but flamin in the high pride of life, drawin the weak and innocent to him. But I never thought; it never came home to me clear; it was all a mystery—when I saw her yonder, in the rhododendron path, runnin away as if she thought I was watchin her. I'd not do that; it was more a anxiousness, unknown even to my own heart. I wondered never to see nobody with her in the Little Wood, and how she avoided me, as if I was a ill sight for a young girl. But I've seen him there; I've looked in his face . . . God will deal with him. He's a great high man above what we can do. But there's justice before His throne, if there's none on earth . . . O Lord, have mercy on the innocent and the poor! Don't let your lambs be forsook; we'll spread our sad news before you, and our weak hands are held up, and we'd hold them higher and cleaner but for our sins . . . The Lord will deal with him!" Paul cried.

He slipped upon a sudden from his chair on to his knees, and began to pray. He prayed as Mrs May had never heard man pray; the vehemence of his words and manner frightened her, and she trembled as she sat watching him. She could not understand all he said; it seemed to her that much of it was in an unknown tongue. He closed his eyes and clasped his great hard hands, and his limbs shook as though he had lost control of them. He shouted out his petition in a voice that was quite unlike the voice of his ordinary conversation. He was never still a moment while he prayed—now his folded hands were lifted up, now unclasped as he knelt almost prostrate; now his arms were stretched forth as if to ward off the attack of some invisible adversary; and continually as he writhed, he prayed, till he was overwhelmed by the violence of his emotion.

"Paul, Lizzie'll hear," Mrs May whispered. She took hold of his arm to stay him, unable longer to bear the sight of this. "Lizzie'll hear, Paul. She's stopped cryin. She'll have heard what you've said, Paul."

When he opened his eyes he was so exhausted that he seemed to see nothing, and was apparently incapable of rising. It was as though his body and soul were parting. Mrs May took a cup of water from the table, and offered it to him, but he shook his head; and she, having helped him into his chair, wiped with her handkerchief the sweat from his face.

"Paul, you're shakin all over. What's come to you?"

"There's been an answer, Mrs May," he said.

"What was it, Paul?" she asked, more to humour him than from belief that anything supernatural had happened in her little room.

"The answer was, there's been wickedness done, and sufferin must come—I donno who or what—but somebody'll have to suffer. It wasn't showed to me plain; I couldn't have bore it—but there must be sufferin. This that's been done must be washed out with pain. I saw a red fiery flame, and that means violence, more wrongdoin it might mean—mebbe to cover and hide up what's been done . . . Nothin was clear as to that . . . His ways is unsearchable and not to be found out till our hearts is broke and subdued. Ay, there's been sore wickedness, the voice said, and the wrath must be appeased."

Mrs May crouched at the Prophet's feet, holding his hand.

"Oh, Paul, Paul! you say violence—bloodshed—and it's that weighs heavy on me."

"Has it been done? Has aught been done to him?" Paul asked eagerly.

"Not that I know of, Paul. But I fear for what Willie might be tempted to do when he's told about Lizzie. He loves her as brothers don't often love their sisters. It's beautiful to see the love and care he has for her, and he's not differed any since he got married and had children of his own. But Willie's sich a headstrong passionate man, there's no knowin what his passions may lead him to when the shame of Lizzie's trouble is upon him."

"He mustn't be told," Paul said.

"His wife suspects."

"Ah, women do first," Paul said. "But you'll have to try to keep it from him till Lord Lusson is far afield. I'm told he's going to India soon, or some other foreign land, and this'll have to be kept from Willie till he's gone. His passionateness is not to be trusted; I saw him near kill a man once because he said somethin out of the way to his wife. He knocked him down, and when he got up, lifted him off the ground and threw him over a hedge. I was terrified for the poor man's life, and went over to him and helped him on his way. Willie went off with his wife, takin no notice. . . . And his love for Lizzie has always, as you say, been beautiful and proud, and I'd not wonder if it comes near to unhingin his senses when he learns the truth." Paul lowered his voice—" Would you suppose there's aught I could do for her, Mrs May? You're her mother; and you've been a kind and jealous mother, as I've known, though it's been upon me at times that Willie's pride in Lizzie might be a stumblin-block to her. There's many of us needs to be forgiven; it's hard offen to say, when we're wishful of doin what's right and just, whether we're not makin hurt for them that's the apple of our eye. But if I can help in this mournful time, I hope you that's Lizzie's mother will not be backward in sayin what it may be."

"I'm thankful for your words, Paul. But I can't think what can be done. I thought of goin to see Lord Lusson——"

"No, no," Paul said. "Mrs May—Mrs May—you'll not let that man take her away!"

"But what can we do without him, Paul?"

"We can be her friends, Mrs May. If he takes her away, what'll be her life? . . . No, no, no, Mrs May, it's more charity to keep her from him."

"Paul, Paul," Lizzie's mother cried, "it's breakin my heart——"

"Only as his wife," said Paul; "only as his lawful wife."

"But there's no hope he'll make her his wife, Paul."

"Then there's no hope at all from him. It's unpossible, Mrs May. If he was to take her from her home, he'd not find her another —it's not in his nature to; if he'd loved her he'd have had more regard for her good name and the peace and honour of you her mother, and Willie her brother, and her kith and kin. And then, unless her heart and spirit was to break, she'd become blind to high things, and that would be far worse than the finger of scorn in Occlesby."

In the brief silence Paul's eyes again wandered to the bedroom door. The sobbing had ceased; not the faintest sound came from the room.

"Mrs May, I don't want Lizzie to hear. . . . Mrs May, would you think she'd marry me? . . ." Paul held his breath awhile. "You must have judged, Mrs May, that I've loved her for years. I've thought at times she might have guessed it herself, though I've never spoke a word of love to her, not wishin to stop her happiness, and knowin how pretty and clever she was, and like to be sought for by a more presentable man. But if it's different now . . . I donno why . . . mebbe it might be different to some. . . . Mrs May, I hope you'll not think it of me, that I'd presume in a time of trouble—I'm sure you'll not think that, Mrs May, bein Lizzie's mother, and almost the only one that understands me since you laid out my mother for her grave. . . ."

IV

"Paul," Lizzie's mother said, "I'd never think it of you, that you'd take the advantage of them in sorrow, whatever else I might think." She wiped her eyes. "You've showed me many a kindness, Paul, and you've kept our garden neat and tidy since poor father died, and you've borne in patient silence many and many a unkind and misrespectful word from Lizzie, that she could never have meant in the spirit of the words——"

"Ay, I'm sure of that, Mrs May."

"And I've heard her say of you, how good you are, and your gentle ways have often touched her, for all her light words to you. It was not so long ago she said, if you was like somebody else, with your nature, what a fine man you'd be. But I spoke to her about it once—what you've said of lovin her; not sayin it came from you, but from me—and she told me, and I believe it came from her heart, Paul, that she could never marry you, even if she was to be a old maid all her life."

Paul smiled strangely.

"Well, well," he said, "I daresay she's right. A bonny proud lassie like her can't be for sich as me, and it do make me look presumptious on my part. Only, I thought if she cared for me a little, or if there was a feelin within her that she might learn to care for me. . . . But I beg your humble pardon, Mrs May, and Lizzie's likewise, for havin said sich a thing at sich a time, when you can't laugh at me."

"We'd not do that, Paul."

"No; I don't believe you would, Mrs May; nor Lizzie neither, if she thought I was serious. It's not many young ladies that take me for serious at the best, and it offen amuses me when ·I'm alone to think how much they see to laugh at in me. And it'll always been a great comfortable remembrance to me, what you've said she's said about me, and her sayin it shows there's good in her, or she'd never have tried to see it in me. And I do hope no harm's been done me mentionin this, Mrs May."

"No harm, Paul; none at all. It was only your goodness that made you take pity on her."

Paul shook his head. "It's a wonder to me," he said in a low voice, "what them that are kind of heart do think of me. It makes me feel more broken and helpless than harsh words. Ah, there's more kindness in the world than we offen think, when we're took hold off by Giant Despair. Willie pays your rent, do he not?" Paul asked.

"And more than that," said Mrs May. "The rent's half-a-crown a week, and ever since his marriage, Willie's give me another two shillin to keep the house with, he's sich a horror of parish relief for his mother. Lizzie, with her dress-makin, has done what she could, but young girls wants things for themselves that make a hole in what dress-makin brings in. We've managed nicely up to now; though my mind" (Mrs May's lips quivered) "is not easy because I've not watched over Lizzie as a mother should."

"I'd not say you've call to reproach yourself on that account, Mrs May. It was to be—and the end's not yet. But it's very hard and marvellous, this bitterness to come to one so young and bright and free of spirit—and on you, and Willie, and his wife, and your relations in Stanforth, for the worst of wrongdoin is, we can never do it and only suffer ourselves. It's the same with doin good; we're all in a family, and can't get away from it. But we must stand by her, and hope she'll live to lift up her face again in smiles and gladness, for she's but a young lassie yet—not out of her teens—Ay; but a child, and she looks a child, no more. . . . Poor lassie, poor lassie. . . ."

Paul rose, and took his blackthorn and his hat from the floor.

"It's in my mind, Mrs May, to go to this young lord, and ask him to make sich amends as a man should. He ought to be spoke to before he goes away. But I'd not like to do it if it was against Lizzie's wishes and yours."

"I'll speak to her, Paul." Mrs May went towards the bedroom door. "Lizzie," she called softly. There was no answer. "Lizzie —here's Paul Penfold come to see you." Still there was no sign. Paul held up his hand.

"Don't call again," he said.

He made for the door opening on to the garden; there, turning, with the door slightly open, he said: "Mebbe she'll not wish to be disturbed while she's restin. I'll come back in the dusk, if you think there's aught she'd like to say to me. Will you give her my. . . love, Mrs May, and say I'm her friend, and always at her biddin? And God bless you, Mrs May, and God bless and comfort Lizzie ——"

He slowly pulled the door open and went out, putting on his hat when he was in the garden, as though he were leaving a hallowed place.

He was limping down the garden when the cottage door was opened again, and a young girl, with soft brown eyes and plenteous brown hair, stood on the threshold looking after him. The girl was dressed modestly in black: attire which seemed sadly to harmonise with the deep distress of her pretty oval face. Her mother stood behind her, looking over her shoulder.

"Call him back, Lizzie."

The girl sighed, but did not speak.

"He's your true friend, Lizzie. You can trust him."

"Paul . . ."

Paul looked back at once, and the girl bowed her head, and began to weep afresh. Her mother took her by the hand.

"Come in and sit by the fire, Lizzie."

They had gone from the doorway before Paul got to it. He shut the door very carefully behind him. Lizzie was standing with her elbows resting on the chimneypiece, her face in her hands. She was weeping as one who had wept till her strength was spent.

"Lizzie!" Paul said.

She did not move as he approached the fireplace. He stood behind her in an attitude of reverence and humility.

"Lizzie," Mrs May said, "here's Paul come back. Won't you speak to him?"

But the girl would not show her face.

"Oh, mother!" she cried, and sobbed.

Paul had put his hat on a chair, but now he took it up again, and saying in a whisper, "I'll come in the time of dusk, Mrs May," returned to the door.

"He's goin away, Lizzie," Mrs May said. "Surely you'll say a word to him?"

But Lizzie wept the more.

"My dear lassie," Paul said, "you must keep up your heart——" He drew near to her once more. He did not dare touch her; but he rested his hand on the edge of the mantelshelf, and looked upon her with a hungry affection. "Lizzie, it's not in my power to speak the thoughts of my heart. But I'm your friend, Lizzie—ay, you'll believe that, my dear—I'll always be your friend." And then he went from the house, and down the garden, and out on to the hilly road.

V

PAUL, remembering that he had received scant encouragement (and feeling, moreover, a little shaky), did not return to Mrs May's cottage in the evening. It was no way of Paul's to be abroad of nights: sunset, as a rule, drove him indoors, and sunrise awoke him, as though he could hear it telling the glory of God. So, in this still twilight of pain, he shut himself up in his hut (that was set remote among undergrowths on no-man's land, where nightingales every June made the air tingle with fiery song), and there meditated what he should say when he stood face to face with the destroyer of Lizzie's happiness. And Paul, in his loneliness, had a vision of the world's course, and the things men do and leave undone. "It seems naught to them that pass by," said he to himself. He was very, very perplexed and heavy of heart.

But Paul was not to be left alone with his thoughts this evening; for Willie May, going homeward along the Alveton road after a late job at a country house (Willie was a carpenter, and accounted an honest workman), chanced to call at the Prophet's hut —not that Willie sought any favour of Paul, or had suspicion of the trouble brooding over the old home, but simply, so to say, for the sake of calling. As became a strong man of masterful temper, Paul's queer mode of life interested Willie, and amused him. This sort of hermit existence would never have suited Willie, and he held the Prophet in open scorn that he should stand to it year upon year, without murmur. "You're a downright old woman, Prophet," had he said over and over again; but few words harsher than that, for there was sometimes an incomprehensible something about Paul that made Willie pause in his not ill-meant pleasantries to consider himself. Nor was the rough giant angered at this, as a small soul would have been. It must be religion, he confessed to himself, feeling at the same time that he would rather be as he was, and marvelling greatly why good people should so often be weakly of body.

The Prophet, when his visitor came stalking impetuously into the hut, turned up the lamp and gave him hearty welcome. Willie had a straw basket of carpenter's tools swung over his shoulder, and this, in a kind of lordliness of superior might, he flung on the floor, as he sat down on a wooden bench in that corner of the hut where the Prophet had lighted a stove to keep out the damp night air.

"Hooh! there's hardly room enough for two decent-sized men—like me and you—in a toadstool shanty like this," Willie said.

It was easy to believe that he was Lizzie's brother. His mother's word stood for it that he was the handsomest man in the village (now his father was gone), and the claim was not so extravagant as to be scoffed at in Occlesby; it was commonly admitted, indeed, as touching other mothers' sons. The young man, with his dark vivid eyes, strenuous head, and muscular admirable limbs, was of the type that inspires the feminine imagination. His forehead hardly favoured him: a subdued light gave it a vaguely noble outline, but in the daytime could be seen hills and hollows that recorded crude intelligence and passions uncontrolled. Willie, in truth, would have been rather ashamed of himself not to be able to blaze forth when anything put him out. Paul had knowledge of some of his lawless doings, and in past years had feared for what might have been; but Willie's faults (in Paul's estimate of good and evil) weighed but as a feather in the balance with his devotion to his mother and his deep love for his sister, which yet did not cause him to neglect his wife and children. There was none like Lizzie, Willie seemed to think, said Willie's wife. The sisters-in-law had never fallen to open quarrelling as to the heights and depths of their merits in Willie's eyes; though it probably needed small provocation to rouse Mrs Willie to candour in this regard.

"If I was you, Prophet, I'd make the hut bigger. You could soon knock that end out and make more of it. I'd be willin to give you a hand, so's to make some sense of the job."

"Thank you, Willie. But it's big enough for a wee bit of a man like me," said Paul, with a humorous twinkle. He had an open book on his knee, with a sheet of writing-paper on it, covered with pencil marks (the Prophet's handwriting was a thing to see); and perceiving that Willie's eyes were grown inquisitive regarding this writing, he closed the book and laid it on one side. The writing was the heads of the pleadings which Paul hoped to commit to memory, for use when he should go to Lord Lusson; and the last words he had written down were, "When lust hath conceived it bringeth forth sin; and sin, when it is finished, bringeth forth death:" words which had a profound and awful meaning for Paul, and, in the last extremity, he was resolved to utter them solemnly in the young lord's hearing, telling him where they were to be found written for the warning of such as he.

"What have you there, Prophet?" Willie asked, pointing to the closed book. "A love-letter—hey? I do believe it's a love-letter! So you're goin in for a wife—hey—like the rest of us common sinners that can't live alone respectable. Ha, ha, ha!"

Paul took up the book (it was a Bible) and put it under his arm with an evident anxiety that caused Willie to make the hut shake again before his explosions of laughter.

"It's a love-letter! I'll be bound it's the Prophet's first love-letter—that's why he's so scared for me to see it. Pooh," said Willie, with a knowing wink and a grand wave of his arm, "them things is nothing when you get used to it. Nothing! I've writ scores and scores in my time, and I daresay they're more fuller of lies and rubbish than most things in black and white."

"I shouldn't wonder but what you re right, Willie," Paul said with an abstracted air. "But I can't speak from experience, not havin writ them myself at sich a rate. What's in this book is no love-letter, Willie; it's not in that style at all." He patted the end of the book. "No; this is a strong argyment from the Word—a kind of sermon.

Yet not a sermon so much as a explanation; and it's only to be preached to one."

"That'll be a lively sort of religious service," Willie laughed. "I'd like to be there in the gallery, watchin the congregation's face. I hope you'll spare their feelins, Prophet!"

"Willie, Willie—it's not the merry-hearted matter you think. But then, you donno———"

"What's that I donno? Well, I must be off," said Willie, picking up his tool-basket. "Here, while I sit bletherin with you, the wife's bein kept waitin for her supper. Good-night, Prophet."

"Well, good-night, Willie," Paul said, "if you can't stay a while longer. I do like your company sometimes, Willie."

"Sometimes!———"

Paul smiled; he felt a little aggrieved at Willie's manner and the abrupt ending of his visit, and this was meant as a terribly severe sarcasm. He was moving to the door, to open it for Willie (a thing Paul always did for his visitors), when the carpenter took him by the shoulders and gave him a good-natured shaking.

"I'll pay you out for that, Prophet! But, lord, you are a man of skin and bone! I wonder you don't sell yourself to a rag-shop——"

"I'm not ragged, Willie; you can't say that of me, though I'll agree to it, I've no mountains of fat to spare. But where's the hole in my clothes you can set eyes on?"

"Never mind, Prophet; never mind; it was only my joke."

Willie got outside rather hurriedly; then, wheeling round, and laughing a little self-consciously, he held something above his head.

"I've got your blackthorn, Prophet!"

"Oh—but you mustn't take it," Paul said in a meek, persuasive tone. Willie, as he backed himself from the hut, continued to laugh in a forced, shamefaced way; and Paul felt glad that he did not seem to be proud of his cunning in surreptitiously seizing the walking-stick. "Now bring it back, that's a good lad"—for Willie kept moving away.

"It'll be all right, Prophet! You'll get it again when I'm tired of it. You're strong enough to do without a crutch at your time of life!"

"So are you, Willie."

"But I want it; I said to myself, I must have the Prophet's blackthorn, and now I've got it fair and square!"

"Not fair, Willie——"

"Ha! but *you* couldn't have stopped me if you'd seen!"

"Willie, I want my blackthorn. There's not sich another in Occlesby——"

"Ho!" cried Willie, "there's carnal pride in a man of religion. He's got the best, and wants to keep it! I'm ashamed of you, Prophet; you're as ungodly as the rest of us!"

"Willie, I want my blackthorn!"

"No, no, man! It's far over good for you. I'll keep it out of your temptation; it would sure to be your spiritual downfall!" And Willie disappeared under the trees.

Paul, standing in the doorway, looked out upon the shadows. For some minutes he waited and watched. But Willie did not come back.

"I never would have believed it of him, that he'd do sich a thing," Paul said to himself sadly. He shut and barred the hut door, and went back to his stove and the notes of his sermon for one. He had turned up the lamp in honour of Willie's visit: now he lowered the flame, to save oil. "No," he muttered as he opened the book and spread out the sheet of writing-paper, "I never would have thought it of Willie, if anybody else had said it. Never. And him Lizzie's brother. . . ."

VI

BUT soon, seated alone with his thoughts (which were not always unpleasant companions), Paul forgot all about his beloved blackthorn, and fell into compassionate concernment towards the sorrowing women in the cottage down the hill. He kept the "heads" of his appeal to Lord Lusson on the open book on his knee, and held a half-inch of grimy pencil in impressive literary style between his thumb and forefinger; but this was from mental preoccupation, for he made no addition to his notes. He turned presently to the last chapter of Ecclesiastes, that saddest piece of writing (surely) in the world, and read it out loud to himself, shaking his head solemnly as he paused with his finger at this verse or that. The iteration of the word "broken" in the verse beginning, "Or ever the silver cord be loosed," had a significance for him, on this still night, such as it never seemed to have had before. The fact that he did not understand the chapter simply as a description of old age, was evidence no doubt of the poverty of Paul's mind. But then he was "no scholar:" even Willie May, himself illiterate enough, had a contempt for the Prophet's reasoning powers; and the critical faculty was hardly a thing he would have cared to keep alive. What he did understand was that the chapter called him out of himself into a finer harmony with suffering humanity; and as he left the matter there, desiring to know no more, you will perceive that he was a very ignorant, simple fellow, and not at all a Bible student of the schools.

There was little enough of beauty or of luxury in the Prophet's hut. The coloured texts on the walls would have set a cultured theologian's teeth on edge. He slept at nights—and, he said, soundly, even when storms raged—on a hard straw mattress, covered by a blanket (which was taken to Mrs May every spring to be washed) and an amazing patchwork counterpane of Paul's own making. Then he had a couple of plain wood chairs: to one of which was fastened with string an ancient cushion, this never being used by Paul himself, but reserved for the womenfolk who sometimes dropped in, either from pity or curiosity, or both. The bench near the stove was for strangers, and many a travel-soiled wayfarer had been entertained sumptuously in this secluded abode among the trees. An old trunk containing Paul's Sunday clothes and certain other family heirlooms stood at the foot of the bed: and ever since the marvels of this trunk had been displayed on a memorable occasion to an Occlesby youth of sarcastic wit, it had been celebrated in the region round about as the Prophet's pawnshop. Nobody, it was supposed, save this favoured young man, had ever been privileged to peep therein, and since he was of a somewhat imaginative turn, and given to the study of enthralling literature, it may be that Paul's trunk was not really the astonishing treasure-store reported. Nevertheless, he was an untiring collector of trifles; and when his friends laughed, and said, "Why, you can't have no use for that, Prophet," he would make answer in his quiet, smiling way: "Mebbe no, mebbe aye. There's gener'ly a use for everything if you keep it long enough."

Precious among Paul's treasures were his books; these half-score volumes, all of venerable aspect, were set out in imposing array between two slabs of varnished wood (a Christmas gift, this bookcase, from Willie May), which were fastened together with stout cord, and hung from a gigantic nail which Willie had driven into the wall near the stove, so that the books might not get damp. Three of the volumes were poetical—Shakespeare, Milton, and Cowper (the Prophet read Milton oftenest); two gave the experiences of gentlemen who had made famous names for themselves in the mission field; and the others were more or less religious in tone, including a bulky volume of irregular numbers of that interesting and improving periodical, "The Holiness Testifier," price one half-penny weekly. These honest and sober books were held in affectionate regard by Paul for two reasons; because they were founded on fact, and if not founded on fact (he had doubts about Shakespeare), then because of their wisdom; and because they had all been handled, and some of them even read in places, by his mother, whose memory was to Paul one of the sweetest of the gifts of life. She had not been a perfect woman, and they said in Occlesby that her death was a blessing to Paul, and a happy release to herself; but she had become very beautiful and blameless in the alchemy of his love and gratitude, and he often walked and talked with her still on dreamy evenings in the Little Wood. Paul's Bible was never put in the bookcase; he kept it under his pillow. In it was written, in ink now faded, "Sarah Penfold." Penfold was his mother's "maiden name." Another valued belonging was the silver watch of very considerable dimensions which Paul carried about with him in a deep pocket in the inside of his waistcoat; and when, his chest beginning to ache owing to his remaining so long in a bent position, he now unbuttoned his waistcoat and drew up this substantial and eccentric timekeeper from the depths, he was surprised to find that it was past nine o'clock. He rose, stretched himself, then turned up the lamp a little, and took from the top of the stove a coarse basin covered with a plate. This plate being removed revealed a mess of porridge, sluggishly bubbling. It kept on bubbling after it was taken off the stove, as if the stuff had life in it, a thing that awoke in Paul almost daily wonderment. Drawing his chair up to the small square table (another of Willie May's presents), he stirred the porridge with a wooden spoon, and was deep in the enjoyment of his supper when he was disturbed by an unusual occurrence. Some one was calling his name from without.

"Paul!"

He had heard no noise till his name was called. The voice sounded thick and gaspy, as from the bowels of the earth. It was more like a woman's voice than a man's, but the Prophet could not feel sure as to the speaker's sex.

"Paul!—Paul!—"

This time the voice came clearer, and he recognised it as that of Mrs May. He stood up and looked about him; his visitor was plainly not at the door, and he failed, in the surprise and abstraction that were upon him, to identify her whereabouts.

"Paul—Paul—Paul Penfold!" the voice called out again in a kind of choking frenzy.

"Is that you, Mrs May?" said Paul, staring nowhere in particular.

"Yes, Paul! I'm here—at the window. Can't you see me, Paul?"

"Ay, ay, I see you now, Mrs May." He stepped across to the window, the blind of which he had forgotten to pull down, and stood there looking out at the white distracted face disclosed faintly in the lamp-light. There was a background of willows, and beyond that, a dark purple sky, and one golden star.

"Paul, can I speak to you a minute, if you're alone?"

"To be sure; to be sure, Mrs May. I'm all alone." He motioned with his hand for her to go to the door, and went and opened it. "Come in, Mrs May, come in," he said reverentially.

VII

HE stood on one side, and Lizzie's mother glided into the hut as though she were some conscience-stricken wretch escaping from justice. She was dressed in black, and the black shawl over her head was held to her throat by fingers that were like the fingers of one dead. Paul made haste to bring her the cushioned chair, the chair of honour that should be for Lizzie's mother more than for the finest lady in the land; and she sank down on it, sighing, sighing, and pressed her hand to her side. The expression of her face told of anguish and grief of mind, and made Paul's heart beat fast with sympathy and fear. He shut and barred the door.

"Mrs. May, it's Lizzie . . . Mrs May, you look as if you'd seen a ghost!"

He turned the other chair and sat before her; and as she did not speak, he leaned towards her and just touched the hem of her shawl, lifting it gently on his forefinger with a significance of pity more profound than any words that were possible to him.

"It's Lizzie, Mrs May. . . . She's left her home . . ."

"No, Paul—no. It's worse than that, Paul . . . Lord Lusson's dead!"

"Dead!" Paul said. "Lord Lusson——"

"Paul, Paul, Willie's took his life!" Mrs May murmured, and hid her face in her shawl, shivering from head to foot. And after that there could surely be no more poignant silence than the silence which fell on this little hut among the trees.

"Mrs May . . . Mrs May . . ." Nothing more could Paul say; his mind was suspended. But he began again to utter her name, as if that were a comfort to him, and to her, and his hands moved pathetically, like one trying to find his way in the dark. And then—"Ay," he said strangely, "he was the kind that would make darkness his secret place. Mrs May, Mrs May! this is the Lord's doin, and it's wonderful in our eyes, and past findin out. It's His answer, though not as we thought, and there's to be more sufferin. . . . His ways is not our ways, and He's able to mend evil by seemin evil, and make us run to Him for pity and mercy . . . when the pavilions of the wicked is broke down by the swift angel He sends . . ."

"Oh, Paul, Paul! . . . My Willie; my poor Willie! . . ."

The mother was not weeping: her soul was drenched with tears, but her eyes were dry. She showed her face a moment, and Paul gazed upon her as if she were in a sickness unto death. Then, as she bowed her head almost to her knees, her thin gray hair fell out from under the black shawl on to her brow, and Paul smoothed it back with an indescribable reverence. One white hair stuck to his finger, and he took it off and laid it on the Bible, a sacrifice of exquisite pain. He closed his eyes a moment, and said to himself: "I donno what to do, but I'd be thankful to share her burden." The sense of her isolation, and of his, oppressed him, and made him feel how little after all one soul can do for another.

"You say Lord Lusson's dead. But—you're sure, Mrs May?"

"Oh, yes, yes, Paul! Willie took his life only half an hour ago. He came back home to tell me after he'd done it. And now he's gone away, leavin his wife and children and me for ever. 'You'll never see my face again on this side the grave,' he told me . . ."

"It's unsearchable," said Paul. He took on to his knee the basin containing the remains of his supper, and began to stir the porridge with the wooden spoon. "I'd look on it as a favour, Mrs May," he said, " and a honour to my cookin, if you'd try a helpin of this. You're not over strong at no time, and you've suffered more than a woman should this day. It's a supportin food, Mrs May, though not dainty for every taste, I suppose; and you look as if you was in need of sustenance, if you'll not take it amiss me sayin it."

He poured into the basin the rest of the milk, which he had been saving for his breakfast, and turned the spoon in an inviting way, saying: "If you'll try this, Mrs May, I'm sure it'll nerve you wonderful; it does me, I know, when I feel a bit weak and wore. It's the best I've to offer, and I've offen had better in your house, where I've never lacked for a supper or a cup of tea when I've been in need of one." Mrs May did not speak, and did not look up, and Paul rattled the spoon gently on the rim of the basin to attract her attention. "Mrs May, will you not taste this fine porridge that's my own makin? It's been on the stove since mornin, so there's no fear but it's proper boiled."

But the mother of Lizzie and Willie shook her head.

"I've no appetite left, Paul," she said.

"Just a mouthful?"

"No, thank you, Paul."

"Then you'll take courage of heart, and tell me what's happened. You see, though I believe somethin's wrong, I can't hardly bring myself to think as Willie's done what you say. But if Lord Lusson's gone before his Maker, I say, howsoever it came to pass, it's the Lord's doin', Mrs May. But Willie was here at dusk, on his way home from work, frank and free and full of his big laughter as ever, joking about my blackthorn.... He took it for a lend ... ay, ay; but it's always like that—a laugh and joke one minute, with sorrow and tears the next. All this," said Paul, "comes to show what poor things we are, and as helpless as little children, nothin being worth, and mysterious to ourselves. But Willie, how did he get to hear of his sister? He knew nothing when he was here, or he'd have behaved different. I was full of anxious thoughts while he was talkin so cheerful, knowin the passionate fierce man he is when you cross him."

"Lord Lusson writ Lizzie a letter, that came soon after you left this afternoon, and, foolish like—oh, I've not known what I've been doin all day, Paul—I left it on the chimney-shelf after Lizzie'd given it to me to read, and Willie comin in for a chat, found it there, and read it before I could stop him. Then he understood everything at once, and I hardly knew him for my own son, for the change in his face, and the shrunken look upon him. Oh, Paul, my thought was, the shock of Lizzie's trouble has broke down his mind!——"

"Very like, very like, Mrs May."

"And then he had one of his fits of passion, worse than I've ever seen him. I was thankful Lizzie was out . . . the wild things he said. He wouldn't believe my word she wasn't at home, and went to her room to look, and came out shoutin like a madman, she's gone to meet him in the Little Wood, and ran out of the house. . . . He came back, I donno how long after, lookin wilder than before, and when he said he'd killed Lord Lusson in the wood, I pulled him to the window and looked at his hands, and when there was no blood on them, I said to him, no, no, Willie, you've not done it, but he vowed he had, and said he wasn't sorry he'd done it, and would do it again if he was alive and cumberin the ground."

"Where was the place," Paul asked, "the young man writ to Lizzie to meet him?"

"The rhododendron walk."

"Then these secret meetin's is why he's had it closed——"

"She was to be there at half-past eight, and it was when she was gone that Willie came, and I've not seen her since. I suppose she'll be wanderin about the place waitin for him. . . . When Willie came back the second time he only stayed a minute, to say good-bye for the last time, and as soon as he was gone I ran up the hill to tell you, for I couldn't abide in the house for my thoughts, with no light, the lamp havin run dry. . . ."

Paul took her hand. "You'll be of good cheer, Mrs May. It's not positive certain Willie's done this great sin. Did he say aught how he done it?"

"No, Paul. He only said it, then took me in his arms and kissed me, like as he's never done before, and said God bless you, mother, but never a word of blessin or cursin for Lizzie, and he'd never see me again on this side of the grave, for he wasn't going to disgrace his family by lettin them hang him. . . ."

"Have you the letter Lord Lusson writ to Lizzie?"

"Yes; it's in my pocket."

"Would you care if I was to read it? It may help in my ideas."

Mrs May handed him the note. Paul, being a little short-sighted, held it close to the light.

"DEAR LIZZIE,—Do you think you could find time to run up to the rhododendron walk about half-past eight to-night? I am deeply grieved for you. But I hope you will understand how foolish it is to take this trouble so much to heart, and I assure you I shall do all I can for you, and at any rate, if you will keep quiet, and be the sensible girl I believe you to be, you need never want. I should like to call on you, but think it best not to do so, as it might create scandal, which I am anxious, as I daresay you are, to avoid. But we can talk the matter over quietly to-night, and arrange what is best for you to do. You need have no fear of being seen, as I have had the rhododendron walk closed.—Yours, L."

The Prophet read the note a second time: then shaking his head, laid it on Mrs May's lap.

"I don't want it, Paul; best put it over the lamp," she said, glancing affrightedly about the hut.

"I think, for Lizzie's sake, you're in the right," Paul said. "I'll burn it in the stove." He lifted the lid and dropped the letter in upon the red glow. "Now, it's my way of thinkin," he added, "that somebody should make speed to the rhododendron path, and make sure what's happened. If Willie's frighted himself away after only woundin the young man, then he'll need doctor's help, and if he's lying unsensible somewhere off the path, Lizzie might never find him, or know there'd been a quarrel, and he might lie all night and perish for lack of timely aid. I'm but a slow coach myself——"

"Oh, Paul, I could never go there," Mrs May broke in, misunderstanding him.

"I don't say you should, Mrs May. No, no; it's a man's work, if there was a proper man to do it. I'm not commonly considered sich, and I know I'm a sort of snail with its house on its back when I'm on my legs, but nevertheless I'm willin to go and see if aught can be done."

"Will you, Paul?—will you?" Mrs May asked eagerly.

"Ay; this very minute." He hobbled to the window and looked out. "There's the moon full out, with a clean sweep for her over the sky, so that'll be helpful. There's always somethin to be thankful for," he muttered. "We have our cross one minute, heavy as lead, and then a power awakes, and the burden's lighted." He turned to Mrs May. "Now, we'll not talk any more about this, makin sorrows out of mystery, thinkin what may have happened, or what mayn't. But you'll make for home, and I'll slip along to the Little Wood, and however it may be, bad news or good—and I'm in the hopes of good—I'll come down to you before goin to bed, and let you hear the truth of the matter." He put on his hat and turned down the lamp; immediately, however, turning it up again. "I'd almost forgot. You've no oil. See here, take this can; there's a plenty in my lamp; I filled it before I lighted it at dark, and I can get some more in the mornin."

"I can't take the last of your oil, Paul."

"Ay, ay; you must. You'll see sich a anger I'll get in if you don't! Why, it's unpossible for you to sit in the dark a night like this—and Lizzie may have returned when you get home."

He wrapped the oil-can in paper, and Mrs May concealed it under her shawl.

"You're always so kind, Paul."

"I donno about that," said the Prophet. "It's a deal easier to do a little kindness, than not, for them that's unhappy."

He opened the door. They went forth into the calm, beautiful, moonlit night. Paul left the hut door unlocked.

"It's almost like day," he said. "Them with strong eyesight could read print in this light. It's wonderful truly, the comfort in this pleasant white light in the night-time. There's nothin been forgot for us," said Paul. "What we can't find for a peaceable life it's because we pass it by, like butterflies in their crazy rushin over fields of flowers."

Paul slightly leading the way, they crossed among the bracken lying between the hut and the plantation, all the vegetation they touched being wet with dew. They then passed through the plantation, and so on to the highroad. The sudden scampering of some wild creature from its resting-place so shook Mrs May, that she came to a standstill, and could not go on for some moments.

" Paul," she whispered, clinging to his arm, " I feel as if the hand of death had been laid on me this night."

" You mustn't let down your heart, Mrs May," he said.

They reached the by-road which led down to the widow's cottage. Willie's house was nearer, higher up the hill, and Paul saw a light shining there. But of this he made no remark.

" This is your road, Mrs May, and you must go home direct, and leave what's to be done to me. If I was you, if Lizzie's come home, I'd not tell her what Willie said;

there's no call to frighten the poor lass, and if what Willie says is true, she's like enough to hear of it as soon's needful."

"It'll break her heart—and his wife's," Mrs May murmured wearily. "Mine is broke already."

"And as I said," continued Paul, "after I've made search to satisfise me, I'll come down and let you know how it may be with the young man; and even if I don't make no discovery, still I'll come. So you may depend on me."

They stood together a moment, hand in hand, the silent sad trees around them, the gray dusty road under their feet, the white moonlight upon them like a robe of pity.

"You'll try to be brave, Mrs May. And if you'll remember where it says, 'I will never leave thee nor forsake thee.' . . ."

"Yes, Paul."

Her hand was like ice; his also was very cold. She drew so near to him that her shoulder touched his. Finally, their hands fell apart, after a last pressure from Paul's which made Mrs May feel as though a second son had been raised up to her as the solace and protection of her old age.

"Mrs May, I could almost wish—if it's not a sin havin sich a wish—that I was in Willie's place this night. He's everythin to you, and I'm of small account in Occlesby." And when she looked into his eyes, Paul made haste to add:

"I mean, I'd like to bear some part of the burden that's fallen on you, Mrs May. I'm so lonely, you see—yet not lonely in one way neither—and if it was me that had done it, whatever's been done, then the sufferin would be less heavy on others, for nobody would grieve much what the law would do to me, a childless and motherless man."

". . . Paul, Paul, you mustn't go to the Little Wood to-night!" Mrs May cried.

But Paul shook his head. "Ay, I'll go," he said.

"No, no, no, Paul!—You mustn't go to the Little Wood!"

She gripped hold of his hands, and appeared to be falling down before him; and Paul, fearing that she might become too weak to go home alone, put his arms round her, and held her as in a lover's embrace. He kissed the black shawl that covered her head.

"Ay, ay, I'll go, Mrs May," he said. "It would be a happiness. . . . But I'm keepin you in the cold. There, that oil-can's fell— my clumsy doin. No; the cork's not come out: I knocked it in firm for fear it should, and spoil your clothes. . . . God be your guidance, Mrs May——"

And Lizzie's mother, drawing her shawl over her poor wrecks of shoulders, glided down the hill.

VIII

THE Prophet, trudging along by the side of the Little Wood, made for the rhododendron path. He walked, considering his mission, with even more than his usual deliberation; and the awkwardness of his gait was such, that an impulsive hasty person swinging past might have deemed him injured, or at least sore of limb. The truth was, he missed his stout and sure old friend the blackthorn walking-stick to which Willie May had lawlessly helped himself. In the moonlight it was not so difficult to get along pretty safely. But the broad belt of shadow, fancifully pointed and frayed, that was at times cast from the trees into the middle of the road, was in places thrown right across the game cover on Paul's left, and then, unaided by his blackthorn, it was not so easy to make headway among the shadows, for the road had no pathway, and was full of surprises in the way of holes and cart ruts. And the peril of these was increased by the impulse to keep looking up to the sky, which was this night so strong upon the Prophet. Every now and then, even where the moonlight failed to touch the ground, rabbits pattered across his path, and at such times Paul would be suddenly recalled to himself, and remember that he was tramping a more or less precarious woodland road, where at any moment he might be tripped up, and measure his length on the ground. But these periods of clear comprehension of his surroundings were but momentary; and for most part of the way, after leaving Lizzie's mother, his eyes were fixed on the heavens. It may be that he saw there more than was actually to be seen: more than men customarily see, looking skyward on a moonlit night with the naked eye. He did not care so much for the miracles of tranquil loveliness around him, as for the signs and wonders which he saw, or thought he saw, writ in the dark purple sky. It may be (for the absolute thing cannot always be said of a man like Paul) that the wondrous heavenly beauties he beheld were to some extent the creations of a pure heart and an imagination simple as a child's. He had the gift of wonderment; Paul never grew old, never understood the mercilessness of the forces that make for power. And being lamentably unscientific, he was quite in the dark as to the physical structure of this radiance overhead, this stupendous purple arch with stars innumerable set in the midst thereof. He felt humbly bewildered as to how it came to pass that the stars should be of different colours, some of bright shining gold, with sprays of golden light shooting out all round them; some blue as the feathers under a jay's wing; some red like fire (these inspired especial awe in the Prophet, making him think of the wrath of God as Isaiah and Jeremiah have written concerning it), and others as white almost as the whiteness of the moon—how all this came to pass he knew not, nor would have asked the wisest man living. And the arrangement of the stars also caused him much silent perplexity and awe-struck admiration. They were set forth in many ways, in many forms; and each star-shape, he did not doubt, had its own spiritual meaning. Paul did not find it hard to believe in the supernatural.

When he got to the gate opening on to the rhododendron walk, and lifted the iron latch, he found that the gate had been nailed up. As he stood, thinking things, he perceived the notice-board about trespassing which Lord Lusson had had put up. Willie, then, had made himself a trespasser: and Paul was going to do likewise, yet without any prickings of conscience. He was compelled, the gate being hazardous to climb, to force his way through the beech hedge.

He moved slowly into the interior of the wood. It was darker here, and in the tremulous light that came down through the branches of the trees the huge rhododendrons rose on either side of him like green-black walls. It was as though he were walking in a ravine. The pathway, in contrast with its towering dark borders, showed like chalk

covered with a thin layer of red soil. The
Prophet no longer looked heavenward: for
one thing, there was nothing to see but
gleams and broken patches of moonlight;
and now more terrestrial thoughts occupied
his mind. He walked almost noiselessly.
Not a leaf stirred: not a bird or other living
creature moved; the silence was absolute.
Only the stars, seen for a moment at rare
intervals, the trees, and the gleams of moonlight seemed to be conscious of his presence
in the wood; for inanimate nature was not
beyond the frontier of Paul's charity. He
had advanced perhaps fifty yards, and was
still keeping to the path, when his foot struck
against something lying on the ground, and
stooping, he discovered with much surprise
and a certain mournful gladness, that this
was his own faithful blackthorn. He picked
it up and went on his way, saying to himself:
"Poor Willie; poor Willie. . . ."

His steps were surer now, and he exercised
a greater vigilance. He made better use of
his ears than of his eyes. At places, such
was the darkness where the foliage was thick,

he could scarce see farther than a yard or two before him; but at other times he could make out the trunks of the trees, and occasionally, where there were gaps in the rhododendrons, he could see some considerable distance into the wood. Once a peculiar rustling sound, as of someone moving with difficulty through undergrowths, broke in upon his hearing; and this brought Paul to a sudden standstill. But though he stood listening for a minute or two, the sound was not repeated that he could hear, and he concluded that it had not been caused by a human being. It made him think of Lizzie; but it seemed to him that she must have gone home. He felt, indeed, that he was the only living mortal in the wood about here.

When he had reached what he judged to be the middle of the wood, he left the path and went in under the trees. The darkness was upon him heavier than ever now, and his tread was soundless. He moved about like his own shadow. This even occurred to him — that he was his own shadow; and he smiled at the fanciful notion.

He went on and on. To a craven spirit it might have been a fearsome quest; but fear the Prophet had none, of man, or devil, or death. Yet there was a certain eagerness upon him as he wandered about at random, in apparent repose of mind, knowing not at all where to look, where to go, but trusting merely to chance; and hoping that he might have to search till daylight in vain.

He kept his eyes on the ground for most part, and continued to move about in different places. That was all he could do; unless he called upon Lord Lusson by name—and this Paul shrank from doing. He would be sure to hear the faintest moan. At length he got quite out of the way of the rhododendrons, and could form no impression as to the part of the wood into which he had wandered. He guessed that he was getting nearer to Lusson Place, the private grounds of which came up to the Little Wood on the west, where there was a venerable yew hedge. Coming presently to a clump of undergrowths of singular formation, Paul no longer felt vaguely lost, but knew that he was within a stone's throw of the gardens. Here the trees did not congregate so thickly together, the light of the moon being therefore let in more freely. Indeed, there was at this spot a considerable irregular circle, which was as clear to stand in as though one were in the open country. Feeling a little tired (his bed-time being long past), and perceiving the gray-mossed trunk of a larch lying prone on the ground, the higher part of it hidden among the underwood, Paul, saying to himself, "I think I'll rest a while," sat him down on the tree, and taking out his watch, consulted its enormous dial. It wanted just a minute to the quarter past ten. "I must have been seeking in the wood for near an hour," Paul reflected. He sighed, and let his watch drop into the deep pocket again, remembering as he did this how Willie used to call it the Prophet's turmit.

IX

AND then suddenly he looked up, and with set lips and fixed eyes, strained his sense of hearing to an intenseness that was a new experience in his uneventful life. But, if noise there had been, the most perfect silence again prevailed. " It was as like to the pushing aside of branches as I've ever heard," the Prophet said to himself. " Ay, it was truly; though I suppose I must have been mistook." He got on to his feet, and was going away, when a strange something, lying in the shadow near the far end of the fallen larch, arrested his attention. As he stood stockstill, gazing at the dark uncertain thing on the ground, a dread touched his heart that seemed to make it stop beating—and at that moment he heard again, or fancied he heard, the same sound as of the faint movement of leaves and the cautious parting of low-hanging branches. But this noise, and the suspicion awakened by it, passed speedily from his mind. His whole attention was concentrated with a dreadful fascination on the dark object clothed with shadow. It appeared to be a thing at once of life and of death, and it made Paul feel that he was in the immediate presence of the supernatural. At last he went towards it.

"The Lord's will be done," he muttered in awe—for he stood by the body of Lord Lusson, and knew that Willie May had done the wicked deed he had said.

For a while Paul was threatened with some sudden and mysterious malady that might leave him grovelling on the sward, unable to speak or act until the seizure had run its course. He clenched his hands till the nails sank into the palms, and by sheer force of will kept off the incomprehensible prostration that had begun to creep in upon him. This he did, not from fear of unconsciousness, but for Lizzie's sake, and Willie's, and Willie's mother; knowing also that light is given to a man whose way is hid. His blackthorn had fallen from his hand, and he did not take it up. He went down on his knees beside the young lord's body, and peered into its face. "Lord Lusson . . . Lord Lusson—" he whispered, his lips almost touching the dead man's ear. Then he laid his hands upon the body, and found that it was cold, and already growing rigid. It lay on its right side, with its right arm across the tree, the upper part of the body being slightly raised from the ground by reason of its having gone down over the tree almost at the armpit. The head was thrown back, as in the agony of the last breath, and the mouth and eyes were open. The left knee was drawn up, as a man may lie idly in bed, but the right leg, much to Paul's surprise, was stretched forth straight as a spear upon the ground. Paul could not doubt that death had come to the young man with terrible suddenness.

Ssh ! . . . There, once more, was that same mysterious movement among the leaves ; and the sound this time sent a cold shiver down Paul's spine. He lifted his eyes quickly, and looked about him, and listened, and listened, and thought to make sure by calling out to ask if some one was watching him. But he held his peace. No farther disturbance reached his ears; and his eyes fell again upon the face of the man whom Lizzie's brother had slain. It was an extraordinary circumstance, to Paul's thinking, that no disfigurement should be visible. Certainly he could only see the dead man's face indistinctly; and a handsome, strong, manly-looking face it was, even in death. Yet though he peered down close into it, and even went so far as to put his fingers reverently under the chin and turn the head a little to the left, so as to examine the right side of the face, he could discern no injury save such as might have been caused by the fall against the trunk of the tree. He tried to close the lids of the poor staring eyes, but they were stark, and would not move. He touched the mouth and nostrils, and held up his hand to see if there was blood upon it, but there was none. Then he laid his hand on the young man's hair

... He wiped off the blood on his coat sleeve.

After that, Paul sat on the larch close to the corpse, pretty much (if one may say this) in the manner of a dog keeping watch over a wounded and unconscious master. His eyes dwelt pityingly on the still face, that seemed to be changing as he gazed. Now that he knew the worst a great calm had come upon him: he laid his hand on the cold brow and kept it there for some moments, as if that were all the sympathy he could offer. He recalled the "notes" of the appeal he had intended to make to the man whose glazed eyes now stared out into darkness, and, in his unerring charity, forgot the harsher words he had meant to use, and remembered only the passages of comfort and mercy. It seemed so piteously tragic, the death of this proud-looking young man in the spring-time of his days. "His mother died when he was a boy," Paul said to himself; "ay, I do remember him, a bonny, bright laddie ... And here's what he's found life, a weaver's shuttle ... He's suffered, and there'll be more sufferin before all these misdeeds is called out from the house-tops. More besides him will have to travel the road of pain. Son and daughter, a lone mother, frail and friendless, bowed down and broken-hearted; a young wife and nest of pretty little ones robbed of their bread-winner and the protector of their youth and innocence—for the law, comin with its clock-work vengeance, takes but little thought of the widow and the orphan." Paul stroked compassionately the fair hair. "Poor young man, poor young man, his greatness was of small avail to him. I donno he was worse than many another of his kind, and lower—only, it was to be; it must have been writ against him, and he never saw the writin. As the body suffers, he had less of it at the last than is comin to them that's left in the deluge of this wrath; and there's none to say but what he found more mercy when he opened his eyes on the other side than he thought to find. It would be a awful thing," Paul reflected, "if the world's mercy was all we had to go by."

And then, as the shadows beside the undergrowth seemed to be deepening, the unseemliness of allowing the dead man to lie across the tree in this uncouth position occurred to Paul. The body might become stiffened in this dreadful posture, with its knee drawn up and its arm flung out, and in such case it could only with difficulty, and it might be with mutilation even, be laid in its coffin for Christian burial. Moreover, Paul was moved with a desire to see the face more distinctly than was possible while it was hid in unfriendly gloom.

At no great distance, say twice a man's length or so, from the spot where he kept watch by Lord Lusson's body, the moonlight spattered down clear on the sward, so clear that the dew could be seen shining on the grass. So Paul took hold of the body, under the armpits, and pulled it off the tree. The right arm, with a little pressure, went down by the side, and supporting the shoulders against his knees, Paul succeeded in forcing the drawn leg straight as the other. He tried once more to close the eyelids, but they would not close. All this he did without a shudder, because of his unconcern of death.

Then, holding the body under the arms again, he slowly, moving backwards, drew it over the grass to the spot where the moonlight lay on the grass. He did not pause till he got it there: then, the corpse lying at full length on its back, he knelt at its head with his face over its face. Suddenly, from the undergrowth close by, came a cry that was terrible to hear: a cry that seemed to pierce and shiver the night through all the wood; and the next moment Lizzie May sprang into the moonlit space, screaming out in an agony of terror—

"Paul Penfold! Paul Penfold! . . ."

The girl was as one bereft of reason. She stood with her back to the torrent of white light that poured down from the sky, so that Paul, looking up at her, but remaining on his knees, could not clearly see her face. But he saw enough to feel assured that she knew Lord Lusson was dead. He said no word. He was almost as pale as the corpse at his knees.

"Paul Penfold! Paul Penfold!—You've killed him!—You've killed him!—" Lizzie screamed.

She shrank back, uttering incoherent sounds, and holding her hands in a helpless child-like way before her, as though fearing that an attack was to be made on her own life. And when she got to the undergrowths, she suddenly turned and ran in among them, and Paul could hear her forcing her way in feverish haste through the branches. She appeared to stumble once and fall, for there was a short silence, but the branches rustled and cracked again, and Paul could tell that she was speeding towards Lusson Place. Then, while he could still faintly distinguish the panic-stricken girl's movements, there was a sharp scream, as from physical pain, and then perfect stillness fell on the wood.

Paul, thinking that she had fallen a second time, and perhaps seriously hurt herself, rose up as quickly as he could and hastened after her. When he had gone some way among the rank scrub, which here closed him in on all sides, compelling him to use his hands to clear a path for himself, he heard Lizzie calling, "Help! Help! Lord Lusson's been murdered by Paul Penfold! . . ." as though she had become aware of his approach and was in mortal terror. Paul continued to follow; but presently, getting out of the scrub, and seeing nothing of Lizzie, he stopped, and fell upon a profound bewilderment of thought.

It was very dark, just where he stood, darker than at any part of the wood he had yet traversed. But beyond, in the direction Lizzie had gone, he could discern a black line like a wall, and judged this to be the yew hedge which separated the gardens from the Little Wood. If he went as far as this hedge he would be able to see the roof of the home of the Lussons shining in the moonlight. He did not, however, advance. He had become a prey to a species of palsy. His limbs appeared to be failing him. He put his rounded shoulders to the trunk of a tree and leaned heavily thereon. " I wonder if Lizzie's mother will keep silence," he said to himself. " Nobody else knows, and Willie's away, and Lizzie thinks I'm guilty, and if Mrs May will keep silence——" and, his great soul seeming to overpower his weak and ill-formed body, his knees upon a sudden went out before him, and he fell on his face on the leafy soil, breathing as one helpless and stunned. This condition lasted some minutes; and rising painfully, he again leaned upon the tree.

He could now think more clearly. And he knew that the supreme opportunity of his love was come, and understanding this, he felt quite humble, not heroic at all—Paul had none of the dramatic instinct which makes heroism unbearable in obscurity — and a strange expression, that was something of a smile and something of an indefinable shine, came into his face. His eyes grew larger, and brighter, and the lids did not move. In a few minutes he would be surrounded by angry and horrified men, who would seize him, and call him murderer, and cast him into prison. This he knew; and he knew also that when they came for him he should offer no resistance. "Shall not a man be defiled for his brethren?" Paul had seen the Light, and it was for him to follow it, whithersoever it might lead him.

"And then," reasoned this peasant with himself, "I'm but one, alone in the world, and there's a-many that would suffer and be put to shame if Willie was took—a sister as'll need a brother's watchful care, now more than ever, a wife and little ones that Willie loves dearer than his own life, I do believe, for all his sinful violence, a worn old mother that will droop and fret into her grave if she's robbed of his help and his cheerin word in the declinin days of her hard life. Nothin but misery and grief for them all if Willie is took. But if another . . . then they'd be able to keep their two pretty little homes, and when Willie comes back, the old ways would come again . . . and if it was me, and I was offered up in Willie's stead, there's nobody would grieve much, except it was Mrs May, who's always had a heart of pity for me. . . ."

And then there was a rushing confused sound, and dark male figures appeared under the trees. Paul held up his hand, but no one immediately saw him. So he went forth into the greater light to meet them.

"Lord Lusson dead!—Paul Penfold murdered him!" one shouted in a voice of horror.

And men closed in on Paul on all sides, and he was seized and held fast with savage hands, wild eyes peering into his face.

"Paul Penfold!"

"Ay, it's me, Mister Reid," Paul said. "And I hope, Mister Reid, you'll not let your men ill-treat me, for I'm willin to go with you quiet to the lock-up."

X

Now Willie May, at the time of the arrest in the Little Wood, was a league and more from Occlesby. His escape from the neighbourhood, at an hour when most of the villagers were shutting their doors on the night, and while yet only his mother had been apprised of what had happened, was not a difficult matter. Had Willie got into an intricacy with the officers of the law, the chances were but slender that he would have got out of it. If the horrible news of his violence had been noised abroad earlier, and he had been surprised, say in his mother's house or in his own home, during the few minutes he lingered in these places, he would have fought desperately for liberty and life. But the struggle would have been solely physical; for Willie was not at all a man of resourceful intellect, and of the low cunning of innate criminality he had none.

The truth was, in the madness that possessed him, he had no regard whatever before the event to the consequences of his appalling deed. He was under the dominion of elemental impulses, which dethroned reason and trampled it under foot. Nevertheless, when the frenzied man rushed to the Little Wood to seek out the destroyer of his sister's honour, he had some dim notion that he was ascending the scaffold, prepared to die there for Lizzie with a shout. And the instinct which led him to confess to his mother, was the same instinct which in the calmer hours that were to come made him understand that he had done wickedly, and deserved to suffer therefor. His act of vengeance was the monstrous abortion of a noble emotion. His love for his sister had been whirled suddenly to an unnatural height of idolatrous contemplation; and he did not pause to think —if indeed he had ever suspected—that idolatry is one of the most destructive and remorseless forces in human experience.

When, after dealing the swift and furious blow with Paul's blackthorn that ended Lord

Lusson's life, Willie fled from the Little Wood like one demented, he went first to his mother's cottage, telling her, in impetuous incoherent words of the hideous thing he had done, closing her poor shrunken body in his strong arms in the delirium of a love on the threshold of death, she moaning and shivering there as one whose last earthly hope was gone—and bidding her farewell, left her on a chair almost more dead than alive. The dreadful ordeal was over in a moment. Lizzie's name had not been spoken. Willie had not even lingered to caution his mother to keep silence concerning the crime he had committed.

Many gardens were strewn about in pleasant confusion at the back of the cottage in which he and Lizzie were born; and Willie, going where he had no right to be (there was a kind of lawlessness in the man's blood), pushed his way hurriedly on to his home. In impartial moments even the neighbours were wont to say of Willie's cottage and garden that it was the sweetest place in all Occlesby. He was a man who could neither love nor hate in moderation : a man possessing an abundance of idols—and this sweet home, and the modest little wife and healthy children that were set in it like jewels, were of them.

His cottage was somewhat of the formation of his mother's : that is to say, when you opened the front door and went in, you stood immediately in one of the two rooms of the dwelling. When Willie softly entered, the lamp (that had been put on the mantelshelf out of the children's reach) was burning so low that he could only see indistinctly about the little room. He did not shut the door behind him, knowing that he had not come to stay : he pushed it till it stood within an inch or two of being closed. All that was in the room he loved : he had made most of the things with his own hands. It so moved him as he realised that he was looking upon them for the last time that he could scarce bear to keep open his eyes. Susan, his wife, being somewhat poorly in health, had taken advantage of Willie's customary evening visit to his mother to slip into bed, and was already apparently sound asleep, baby by her side. She and Willie slept in the bed in the kitchen, the four older children — all boys, "steps and stairs," as Granny May called them — occupying the big bed in the next room. Baby also was a boy, and there was no idol in Willie's heart like unto this.

He stood looking at his wife.

"Susan," he whispered; "are you asleep, Susan?"

His wife did not answer, did not move in bed, where the lamplight just touched her comely face; and as, with bowed head and drooping arms, Willie made his way across the floor to the bed, he was like a man breaking down from some secret and incurable malady When he got to the bed, he turned round suddenly, and fixed his haggard eyes on the door. Not that he had heard a noise—not that he expected to see someone there. No; but because if he had looked one moment longer upon the faces of his sleeping wife and child he would have awakened them with the poignancy of his grief.

Determining, with vain faith in his powers of endurance, not to let his gaze wander to the bed again, he sat down by the bare table (that was scrubbed white as the driven snow) standing in the middle of the room, and cautiously opening a drawer, took therefrom a sheet of writing paper, and one of those flat, large pencils which men of his trade use in marking wood. The nerves about his mouth were in commotion: his hand was not at all steady. But he managed to write, in such words as he could find, what he had in his mind to say.

"DEAR SUSAN, more falt-finding, and quareling at the shop, I am sike and tird, of it, and the way thats been going on, I have started to looke, for work I dont no whare, but I will find it soe dont, frett dere Susan from youre true, husban, WILLIE MAY."

(For full stops he put commas, and the commas were very large, making the writing look as though every two or three words were in parentheses.)

Now, Willie did not write this note because he thought his wife would be deceived thereby. He did not suppose that for a moment. But he knew that if she were to awake, he could not tell her the truth as he had told it to his mother. He had not anticipated that she would be asleep, and this pencilled note contained the story he had made up in his mind to tell her. He could not tear himself away for ever without passing through the sublime agony of farewell: that, though he knew it not, was part of his atonement; and the wretched man had a vague notion that it was incumbent on him to put into writing the momentarily comforting lie which he had resolved to utter to his wife with his lips.

Having written the letter, he took a fork from the drawer, and leaving the sheet of paper unfolded on the table, drove the fork through it with silent pressure. This done there was nothing else to do, could he have nerved himself to immediate flight. But as he rose from the table, standing up in the black maze of his despair, his throat so swollen that he could only breathe with difficulty, an impulse that would not be governed carried his gaze once more to the bed, and then he discovered that he was being watched by a pair of wondering blue eyes set in a little golden head that was just raised from out its warm nest of bedclothes by mother's side. The father, cringing and trembling, as though these were the eyes of the All-seeing, advanced a pace to the bed. Then he stopped, as in a trance, took a step nearer, paused again—then, tearing out his agony as it were by the roots, he wheeled round swiftly and faced the table once more.

The sight of the note stung him; he saw it now in a different light, saw it as it was, a cowardly mean falsehood; he felt like a living lie, an outcast, a murderer, in the midst of these adorable things of his love. He feared that he must go blind, or scream out, unless he did something. So, averting his face from the bed, he went to the mantelshelf, took down the lamp with shaking hand, and passed into the next room.

Here he found his four boys all sound asleep in bed: the bonniest, bravest boys in Occlesby. And Willie, holding the lamp high so that its light might not fall too strongly on their eyelids, looked upon them for the last time . . . Jim and Harry lying on their backs with their knees like tiny pyramids under the bedclothes: the faces of the other two boys being partly hidden . . . little Paul's brown leg hanging out over the edge of the bed. Willie put it back and drew the patchwork counterpane over it. Then he kissed them all in their sleep, and stole silently from the room.

But baby had been on the look-out for father, having crawled away from mother's side the better to accomplish that purpose; and Willie saw that the blue eyes were upon him when he returned to the living-room, with two fat little hands expectantly fighting the air. There would have been a cry had he not gone to the bed. So at least Willie told himself: though this may have been his unconscious apology to himself for succumbing to the weakness that caused him to tempt his fate. Placing the lamp on the table, he went to the bed and leaned his hip on the edge of it, near to the pillow. He incautiously held his hand before baby's face, and baby made haste to grip hold of the big hard fingers, and before Willie comprehended what was happening, the clever little chap was standing up in bed and saying very plainly that if father did not take him there would be a row. So Willie lifted up the little one in his arms, and baby had soon taken tight hold of his rough black beard with one hand, while the other, in accordance with baby's pretty custom, began to worm its way among the softer hairs down father's neck. And Willie, whispering "Ssh, baby . . . don't wake mumma . . ." the words failing in a low sob, pressed the golden head to his cheek. And then baby, being quick of observation, became concerned with a shining thing, like a raindrop, that had fallen on his hand, and smiling and beginning to crow, held it up to let father see. . . .

XI

THE murderer fled, with his home and his mother, not his crime, uppermost in his mind. He passed the night without sleep, or the desire of sleep. Along heavy roads, over grass and fallow fields, through woods and plantations—so he pushed on, a fugitive and vagabond on the earth, his face towards the uncertain liberty that was certain to be the blackest slavery.

The sense of his personal loss overwhelmed all comprehension of his frightful act. Lord Lusson was dead—but that seemed to be a thing apart. Had it been in Willie's nature to follow the lines of least resistance, he would have gone to the nearest police-station and given himself up. He tried to take hold of his torment and cast it out by sheer physical energy. He carried baby's golden head against his cheek: but it was become lead now — a dead child's head. And when he recalled the last ordeal of the farewell look at his sleeping wife, and her drowsy murmuring of his name as he put back baby by her side, he struck out at the air like the madman he was, and cursed himself, and cursed God, and let his heart overflow with bitterness.

He came presently to this resolve: that he would not let his thoughts dwell on the past. He could not express to himself what it was he meant, but he wanted to tear out his memory and fling it under foot and grind it to nothingness. He partially succeeded in this on the first night of his wanderings. He went on and on like a rushing wind. He never once deliberately looked back, never hesitated in his headlong flight, never let the desire to restore memory touch him with more strength than his sweating body was touched by the shadows of night.

So he trudged till daybreak. Tiredness, scarce recognised by him as such, began to creep on him soon after he heard the early cocks crowing in the cottagers' fowl-houses and the farmyards past which he fled, barely glancing at the shadowy buildings from apprehension that human eyes might be peering out at him from the darkened windows. But it was only when the dawn's rosy flush came up upon the eastern horizon that his pace perceptibly slackened. It was a beautiful daybreak, but Willie saw little of its beauty—of the great black fan that appeared in the east, against a background of purple light that gradually changed and became brighter and brighter of hue until all the sky, from the hills almost to the zenith, blazed with a splendour of opalescent light; then the mighty fan of cloud and vapour, which had meanwhile been spreading itself wider and wider at the wings, though the handle kept shrinking and shrivelling before the burning glory of the sun's approach, began to burst and melt, and become formless; and then came a pageant of colour, a chaos of fantastic shapes, and the triumphant red majesty of day. The spirituality of the dawn had at once solaced Willie and filled him with fear, for day meant the scrutinizing eye of his fellows.

It seemed to him that, although already a long way from home, somebody must recognise him, or that he was bound to betray himself; and then would not the police be sending far and near accounts of his personal appearance? He decided to disguise himself; but could think of nothing more ingenious than the pulling of his hat over his eyes, and an assumed awkwardness of gait. This awkwardness, indeed, was not entirely a make-believe, for Willie, having spent himself in the rapidity of his flight, was beginning to feel footsore and sleepy.

About noon (when he knew not where he was, nor dared to ask any of the wayfarers that came in his path), he stole into an outhouse on the skirts of an apparently deserted farmyard, and, while the sun was brightly flooding the world without, he sank down on some damp straw, and in few minutes was sound asleep. A couple of hours later he was rudely awakened by a bluff old gentleman, with a riding-whip in his hand, and the mantle of perfect health wrapped gloriously about him, and ordered off the premises; and Willie obeyed without a word.

He had taken with him neither food nor money; and he awoke so hungry that, after pushing on for another half-dozen miles or so, he was tempted to stop at the open door of a roadside cottage, and (not caring to beg straight out) asked the good woman of the house whether she knew of any likely work that he might apply for in the neighbourhood. She knew of nothing; work, she told him, was hardly to be got in the district, and several families had been shifting into other countries. Before leaving the door, Willie, his eyes averted in a hang-dog way, shuffled significantly with his feet, looked down on the ground, and mumbled something about hard times—signs of the demoralisation of his manhood, that had set in lamentably after his rousing by the hearty farmer—and the woman, taking compassion on the haggard, travel-soiled man, who appeared to have seen better days, brought him a glass of milk and a bit of bread and cheese. He felt doubly grateful for her kindness, and because she had not forced him to ask for it. He thanked her brokenly: drank the milk; ate the bread and cheese as he went.

In the dusk of the first day, while possessed of a great longing for association of some sort with his fellows, and being moreover dead tired (as one not accustomed to much walking), he lingered about a wayside tavern, where in the porch before the door peaceable persons were gathered together in a kind of awe, paying profound heed to the words of a spruce old gentleman who had a newspaper across his knees and a pair of spectacles high up on his forehead.

"It was my impression," he was saying, "there wasn't a Lord Lusson left in the peerage book, till I read this in the paper. My notion was the title had died out from lack of birth in the proper family, in that line where the peerage was lawful. But here it is in black and white, in our neighbour county too, the most atrocious, foul, dastardly murder. It's not been equalled in my time since that man murdered his two wives, one after the other in succession, four years only between, in the old barn on the Pylstye."

"My grandfather saw him in a cart in his chains," one said.

"This murder is even more horrible in my view," said the spruce old gentleman, "from the lofty rank of the victim. It was done, according to the paper, in the most sudden and diabolical fashion. 'Death,' it says, 'must have been instantaneous.'"

"That's what they say when a man's hanged," another observed.

"Yes; and it's what they'll say when this miscreant assassin is hanged, though a quick choking off is less than his deserts. There ought to be some special punishment invented for him. The blow, from the record, must have been ferocious beyond credit. The fatal place, as near as I can make out, was just here. But I'll read you that part of the account——"

Willie heard no more. Stooping, and rounding his shoulders as if to disfigure himself, he crept away from the tavern. Regaining the high-road, he walked rapidly till nightfall.

It was clear to him that all the countryside

was discussing his crime: a price would be set on his head; his liberty might at any moment be at an end. And now he shunned the villages, slunk past isolated cottages like a thief; he would have died of starvation rather than enter a town just then, his immature imagination not letting him understand that a town would have been the safest place for him. Memory returned, bringing its indestructible torments. He stumbled, in a blinding paroxysm of grief, and fell on his knees on the road in the darkness, and offered his body and soul to Heaven, if only Heaven would take them, and torture them for ever in the furnace of atonement, yet spare his wife, and his children, and his mother. He got up and went on again; and presently passing a sheet of shining ebony, which he knew to be water, the thought of self-destruction came to him, and he stopped a moment. But Willie had been brought up in the Puritan faith, and had the fear of the lake of unquenchable fire before his eyes. He hurried on.

He would keep to his life yet awhile, hoping

against hope that something might happen — a miracle—sudden death by the visitation of God—so that his family and kinsfolk might not have to walk sorrowfully to the end of their days under the intolerable shame of his death on the gallows.

He rested that night under a hedge. The night was fine and clear, but very cold. From the spot where he lay, his head on his arm, he could see, down an indentation of the fields, patches of feeble light. These he knew to be the lights of houses, and they made him wonder what Susan and his mother might be doing. . . .

"And Prophet Penfold," said Willie to himself. "The Prophet 'll not turn his back on them, I'm sure, whoever does." He could not bear the sight of the far-away lights, and held his face to the ground. "The Prophet 'll be awful upset, for I do know how he loves my mother, as if she was his own, and he's been like a older brother to the boys—and to me—they run to him whenever he shows his face. Poor Paul . . . what a strong calm man he seems, back yonder in his hut, wrapped up in his own ways and thoughts. He'll find me in his Bible, I suppose, where he seeks for most everything, and the words to fit it. But he's a merciful man, and when he speaks of me it'll not be over harsh, I do believe—'specially not to Susan and mother."

XII

WILLIE, after that, slept till near the time of sunrise. And as he went along the road again in the first gray waves of dawn he met a country lad whistling gaily to himself. The boy, when he caught sight of Willie, slipt off the road and sallied past on the opposite side of the hedge. He still whistled to himself, though his note was now somewhat tremulously defiant. "What a object I must look when even a boy is frightened to pass me," Willie thought, and smiled grimly. He stopped and called after the quavering chanticleer in knickerbockers: "How long'll it take me to walk to the coast?" The boy turning, moved backwards, and asked what part of the coast he wanted to be at, and when Willie said the seaport—he'd forgot the name—the boy replied he didn't know how far it might be by road to the place where the ships was, but the train fare was four-an-eight there and back if you took a return ticket. Willie thanked the lad, and said that would just suit him. He walked all that day, and slept part of the night under a Scotch fir, so near to a gamekeeper's house that he could hear the dogs barking. A deep-mouthed baying made the fugitive recall what he had read about the uses of bloodhounds.

The next morning broke pleasantly. But soon after sunrise, heavy vapours encompassed the sky, and the atmosphere became strangely oppressive. The oppression increased, and by noon Willie could scarce drag himself along. His brain felt confused, and an acute pain was in his brows. He unbuttoned his coat and waistcoat, and wished there was a breath of wind. Everything—even the sun and the clouds—seemed to be standing still. The trees looked like figures drawn on the horizon: on a common chickens waddled up to him, and immediately, seeing he had nothing to give, prostrated themselves on the parched grass;

a white cat with brown eyes, stretched in a corner that had been scraped bare by the fowls, did not budge as he passed; two horse-dealers slept among bracken, their animals idly grazing; cottage windows and doors stood open, and the flowers looked languid, and the birds were tame and familiar. The stillness was beautiful, yet full of menace. The sky, charged with sulphuric heaviness, seemed to be closing down upon the earth to smother it and all living things.

In the mid afternoon, Willie, the spiritual principle within him grown tenuous and urgent from the keen pangs of hunger and keener mental disquiet, was haunted with the strange fancy that he and the hangman were the only two beings moving in the world. This impression was intensified by his loneliness and the wild and desolate country into which he had wandered. He began to feel the want of tobacco; this punished him even more, for a time, than the want of food; if he had met a fellow-workman he would have asked him for a morsel, and put it in his mouth. A pinch of snuff would have been a comfort. But for a long while he did not come within speaking distance of a single soul: nor did he see a dwelling to which he cared to draw near. And now his feet were like lead when he lifted them, and like fire when he set them on the ground. He walked on turf where he could find it, and this helped him a little. There were intolerable pains in his thighs, knees, and back, and he was getting light-headed. Still he kept his face towards the forest and the low-lying hills that rose up before him in the south against the sullen sky. The hills appeared to be close at hand, but Willie knew that the light was deceptive, and that many miles must be traversed before he could seek the shelter of the forest. When he had passed through the forest, and got over the hills, he fancied that the coast would be in sight.

His course for some while had been barren and drear. But when he was within half-a-dozen miles, as he judged, of the hills, he fell into the way of pleasant and sheltering places. In a lane which had obviously been cut deeper and wider for the convenience of vehicular traffic, although it retained some memorials of the beauty of its better days, a green luxuriance falling over the red crumbling earth on either side, and the scents of vegetation and soil being in the air, Willie was surprised, on going round a bend in the lane, to see an extraordinary kind of man floating down upon him. The man was gazing heavenward : he was a very tall, gaunt person, and came on noiselessly, in a swift, impetuous, aerial fashion, like a spiritualised being who had lost his way from space and was panting and struggling to get back. He carried a white umbrella, and this seemed the only substantial thing about him. Willie edged himself among the verdurous growths to let the stranger pass. But he stopped, and Willie stopped, and the pair looked in each other's eyes a moment in silence.

"Eh?" said the stranger; though Willie had said nothing. He was not at all afraid. The face before him was very pale: the pallor of idealism, and the hair-shirt, and the whip of penance, and the hard bed with the pillow of wood.

"He's like the Prophet," Willie said to himself: "but different."

"I hope you have not far to go," the man said. "The storm will soon be upon us. Look!—it will be a dreadful storm. And you will find no shelter up there—only the trees."

Willie mumbled something about the seaport.

"I want to be there before nightfall."

"Oh, but it is not that way at all. You are quite out of your course. You must come with me, and I will show you. Down here there is a path across the fields, and that takes you to the high road."

They went down the lane together; Willie hastening his pace to keep up with his new friend.

"Have you walked far?"

"Not so very far," Willie said. "It's a tirin' day," he added quickly.

"Yes, we are all tired—some of doing nothing: some of doing too much; some of not knowing what to do. Humanity is crying out for rest, and at the same time growing more and more afraid of it. Aha!——"

A Little Sister of the Poor passed in a pony carriage: the stranger stopped, uncovered his head, and bowed low as the carriage went by. The Little Sister paid no heed to him. "That's the difference," thought Willie; "the Prophet would have felt it, but never have done it, in that ornamental style."

They came to a stile leading to a footpath across fields.

"This is your way," said the stranger. "You seem weary, weary!—get a meal as soon as you can." He closed both his hands on Willie's. "I hope you will find some suitable work presently. Good-bye." He left a sovereign in Willie's hand: rushing away apparently to escape being thanked. Willie held up the money incredulously in his palm, and stood to watch the nervous eager figure and the white umbrella swing out of sight. He brushed something from his eyes as he crossed the stile.

Half-an-hour's walking brought him to the high-road; and another half-hour to a country town, from which (this being market day) farmers' gigs and carts were rattling, the air resounding with the laughter and merry conversation of the occupants. The sovereign had somewhat fortified Willie's courage: still he had no intention of entering the town, though he was compelled, in his search for a tobacco shop, to go on to its outskirts. Here he came upon a sort of general grocery store, which he entered with as much outward unconcern as he could assume.

XIII

THE shopman was standing behind the counter gossiping with an elderly gentleman of benevolent aspect, who sat on a barrel, with his hands folded plaintively across his stomach. They paid hardly any heed to Willie's entrance. The shopman held the sovereign close to his watery eyes, and rang it on the counter, and tested it between his teeth.

"Of course, he'll be hanged when his time comes," the benevolent gentleman was saying.

"I should think they would hang him!" the shopman said. "It's as good as done: it'll be a waste of money having high-priced lawyers for him at his trial. He's confessed, haven't he?"

"Well, it amounts to that almost, though in actual words he's not said he struck the blow. He offered to go with them when he was caught in the wood, but when he was charged at the lock-up he made no statement, and he's had nothing to say since. Before the magistrates he was dumb, and when he was committed for trial at the assizes he walked quietly from the dock, as if it was a matter of less concern to him than to anybody else, the paper says in the report where his personal appearance is described. It's perfectly clear in my mind they've got the right man. If he was innocent he'd make a fine uproar."

"He's a horrible ugly fellow, they say."

"So the paper makes out. Deformed or something. I shouldn't wonder but what he's of weak intellect. There's usually a twist in the brains of criminals of that stamp, though if the law was to take note of it, none of us would be safe in our beds."

"Hang him without a trial, say I; the fuss that's made of such villains in the newspapers only makes them worse, and tempts others to do the same. I wish I was on the jury that's to try him," said the shopman, hand-ing Willie his tobacco and clay pipe and change.

"Has there been a murder done?" Willie asked. "I've not seen the newspapers."

"Lord Lusson's been murdered," said the shopman pompously.

"And . . . somebody took up for it," said Willie.

"Yes, they caught him almost in the very act."

Willie filled his pipe mechanically. "What's the name of the man they've got?" He kept his eyes on the pipe as he spoke.

"Paul Penfold," the shopman said. "He's been before the magistrates for the last time this morning, and they've sent him to the assizes to be hanged."

The men looked a little surprised when Willie suddenly fell against the counter.

"I've had a long tramp," he said. "I hope I've not damaged your pots, sir, with my clumsiness. Did you say the man's confessed?"

"Not in so many words. But he's the murderer right enough. There's plenty of witnesses to hang him twice over and more. The chief witness was the young woman Elizabeth May, who saw the murderer dragging Lord Lusson's body in the wood, to find a place to hide it, and when she screamed and ran away the scoundrel followed her and would have murdered her the same, it's clear, if he could have caught her. But lucky for her, he's a cripple, and the young woman was too fast for him. She gave the alarm, and Lord Lusson's servants rushed into the wood and captured him before he could make his escape. He had the coolness to ask them not to ill-treat him, and it seems never a one laid hands on him. They found the body, with the marks on the ground across where he'd been dragging it to hide it in the bushes, and also they found the heavy blackthorn walking-stick he had done the murder with. There was blood on it, and two or three hairs out of the poor murdered gentleman's head, where the blow had been struck."

Willie sat on an orange box, and was taking a long time to fill his pipe. He did not speak. He sat in a doubled position, his face almost to his knees, his fingers senselessly pulling the tobacco in pieces.

"Some doubt is felt as to the motive of the crime," the gentleman on the barrel said. "It couldn't have been robbery, seeing he took nothing from the body."

"Oh, a woman's in it as usual," said the shopman. "That Elizabeth May could tell a queer story, I'll wager. She's a bad lot, I daresay, and she'll have to own up when the Crown counsel gets her in their clutches. It's known she was carrying on with Lord Lusson, and nobody doubts that's why she was in the wood, in time to be a foremost witness. This Penfold had a fancy for her, though she seems to have given him no encouragement, and when it became known to him what was going on, he was filled with the mad rage of jealousy. That's the theory of the prosecution, and the police can prove it easy. The evidence is circumstantial so far: nobody saw him strike the actual blow, though Elizabeth May couldn't have been far off when it was done——"

"There now, there now," sighed the kind-hearted gentleman on the barrel. "What a lesson for her as long as she lives."

"This Penfold had been seen prowling about the wood, and Lord Lusson himself complained of him being there without right. He must have been watching and planning his opportunity."

"Doubtless there were faults on both sides," said the elderly gentleman. "The girl is very pretty, and the paper says she wept all the time she was giving her evidence. Poor girl, poor girl, there's whispers she's not seen the last of her sorrows yet. Her father's dead, and it's said the murder has so preyed on her poor old mother's mind that's she gone quite crazy and has to be watched almost as if she was a child."

Willie at last looked up. The shopman stared at him, and then glanced at the gentleman on the barrel. Willie, smiling in a strange way, began to draw at his pipe. He sent forth enormous volumes of smoke, which made the benevolent gentleman cough.

"Smoking's not over convenient in a shop," the shopman reminded him.

Willie did not seem to hear; or hearing, failed to understand.

"Paul Penfold!" he muttered, gazing through the doorway. "He'll be in Danbridge gaol now——"

"Yes, that's where they've got him safe," said the shopman. "And they'll keep him there till he's wanted to be buried in quicklime, so as not even the ashes of his bones will be left in the soil. Then they'll cut the first letters of his name in the wall over the place, alongside the others, and that'll be the last of him in this world. I once saw that row of first letters of murderers' names on the wall of Danbridge gaol, and it did seem astonishing, to think that was all that was left of them—every scrap of their bodies wiped clean out, as if they'd never been in existence. It was hard to believe they ever had, though there stood the record of their crimes, and many more at the cross roads, even more thoroughly forgot."

Willie rose and made for the door.

"Good day to you, gentlemen," he said firmly enough.

But on going out he stumbled, and went down on his knees at the threshold of the shop, his shoulder leaning a moment against the doorpost. His pipe fell and broke; he seemed exhausted. The benevolent gentleman made haste to him, and taking him by the arm, helped him to rise.

"You're not well, my man. You'd better stay and rest a little. Shall I get you another pipe?"

"Thank you, sir—no," Willie said. "It was the pipe that done it, I suppose; I've not had a smoke for so long."

He tightened himself up, smiled, said again, "Good day to you, gentlemen," and went away, turning his back upon the town.

XIV

He walked unsteadily, yet rapidly, burning out the remnants of his nervous energy. "Prophet Penfold took!" he kept saying to himself — "Prophet Penfold goin to be hanged!" He turned up the first road he came to that seemed to lead to the hills; still muttering the same words: "Prophet Penfold took! Prophet Penfold goin to be hanged!"

The night was coming on, and coming with it was a mystery of terror that made Willie's heart quail, though he still kept going at a feverish stumbling pace, still bent his face toward the hills. Conflicting air currents, charged with subtle sulphurous fumes, swept and moaned about him like the hot breathing of unseen creatures. As he mounted the rising ground, higher and higher, the forest he had previously seen came again in sight;

but it was now like an immense black cloud that had lost its way from the skies and been driven athwart the slopes of the hills.

Willie could hear a dull rumbling sound in the direction of the town — a sound as of tumult in the streets there; and he could hear the voice of a man shouting anxiously far away. A curlew was calling on the hills, and its cry seemed to go echoing over all the earth. Willie fancied that Paul in his cell in Danbridge gaol must hear that cry; must hear that murmur from the town; must hear that man's voice calling as one in distress over the fields. Frogs splashed in water by the road side; the water was yellow and turbid; the air fell still one moment, and the next was stirred with warm swishes of wind. Willie knew well enough what these portents meant; but it never once occurred to him to turn back. He would get to the coast that night, or never. It might be never; the paralysis of fatalism was creeping upon him; what way was there out of this? " Prophet Penfold took! Prophet Penfold goin to be hanged!" he continued to say to himself, as one who had forgotten all other words, all other records of the past.

Then another thought cut its way through his frenzied brain. He stopped, turned his face to the town, and trembled from head to foot. "I never said he was innocent—I left them to think he was guilty," he said to himself audibly. But the moment after, he was facing hillward again, and going on faster than before. "When I get safe in a foreign land, I'll write home and say I done it," he promised himself.

He went on and on, and the night scowled darker and darker upon him. His feet were covered with wounds and sores. He was walking literally in his own blood.

When the storm broke the darkness was such as barely to allow of his seeing his hand before him. He felt his way like a man without sight. Now the lightning revealed trees clustering about him; now it seemed to him as though he were reeling across some vast and pathless moor. His mental faculties became scarcely of any use to him: he had periods as of intellectual annihilation; the thunder seemed to crash all his brain away. It was usually after the lightning had dazzled his eyes and driven him back appalled, and in the amazed silences after the thunder had cracked and boomed across the pitch-black heavens, that momentary gleams of consciousness returned to him; and once or twice in such moments he lifted up his hands to the sheets of rain that were driving down upon him, and cried aloud: "Prophet, Prophet! I'll see you righted!—I'll see you righted, Paul!" Then his reason again failed, and his brain became more bewildered than the night itself, though the poor wretch went forging onward, battling like some insensate brute creature against the wind and rain; sometimes, when the lightning wrapped him round as with a garment of fire, he stood motionless, tranced, with eyes as of a dead man, a man struck dead as he stood, and then he would see things that were not in the dark night, and would laugh, not loudly, not defiantly, rather softly and musically indeed; the pathos-laugh that means, "I can't make it out—I'm dead beat—" And the wind, as he laughed, whistled in his mouth, and pierced his eyes, and played at hide and seek among the wrinkles of the insane fixed smile on his face. Then he would plunge forward again, recklessly, deliriously, striking himself against the storm—always that, always facing the gale in its angry teeth, slashing at the wind and rain with his hands, the tempest tearing the clothes from his benumbed and sodden limbs, his beard and the hair of his bare head (his hat had long since been lost) washed flat against his skin. It was amazing that he kept his feet so well. But once he went crashing down on his face on stones and mud; and as he lay there motionless, the storm screaming over him, it occurred to him, in a vivid flash of consciousness, that if he did not rise instantly he would never rise again, but perish where he lay. The next instant he was up on his knees, crying out with remorseful vehemence: " Prophet! Prophet! I'll see you righted!—It was me that done it, and I'll see you righted!" Then he staggered to his feet, and went on once more with the aimless recklessness of delirium. He began now to feel that his heart was failing, and although he imagined that he was about to fall over a precipice, he did not stop. If death was before him, he would advance to meet it. Death was behind him also.

So the fourth hour passed. The thunder and lightning ceased; but the rain continued, and the wind blew stronger and stronger. Here and there stars appeared in the ravines of the driving clouds, and low down in the southern sky a huge, black, slow-moving cloud-crag was tipped with the white radiance of the hidden moon. Willie was still making for the hills, for liberty, for the foreign land where he would confess his crime and set Prophet Penfold free, and himself be accounted a murderer for all time to come in Occlesby, and yet save Susan and the children and his mother from the last unspeakable dishonour of the scaffold. And Lizzie too: he allowed himself to think of her now, for the first time since his flight from home; he choked as he thought of her—Lizzie, pretty Lizzie, poor, poor Lizzie. "Ah, God, if you can't have mercy on me, have some on poor Lizzie!" But though Willie held to his way, and hoped against hope, the night had come, and he felt that at any moment he might fall again, and for the last time. He was grown so weak that his knees were thrust out before him, and his chin rested on his chest as he dragged himself along. He knew not at all where he was, whether on a hill-side, or in a country lane, or near a village, or in the midst of a moor. He was too exhausted to lift his head and look about him. He felt that he was receding from life and sinking into the last awful isolation of the soul.

Toward midnight he put his hand inside his shirt against his heart; for it was borne in upon him that he would not live through the night. "If I had a pencil and a bit of paper I'd write it, to save Prophet Penfold," he said to himself. But he had no pencil and no paper, and the words were never written.

Soon after that, Willie fell heavily on the wet and stony ground. Susan came to him; he saw his boys in bed; his mother . . . and Lizzie . . . and Prophet Penfold . . .

This was a very lonesome place where Willie fell. And it was in the third hour after sunrise, on a radiant morning, that some children, on their way to school, came upon the body of a man lying by the road-side. The children did not think but that the man was sleeping, or it might be "lazying" in the warm sunshine. So, standing apart in excited gigglement, each dared the other to go near and see what the man was doing. "If he should be tipsy," one little girl said, "the cows will sniff him and perhaps bite his ear off." And at this there was laughing and clapping of hands; and a boy whispered, "Let's throw stones at him and run"; and another said, "But if he's broke his leg and can't walk, like my dadda did at Christmas"; and, to make sure, two boys (the one waiting till the other was ready, and both till a third said "Fire!") threw stones at the man lying by the road-side; and when this was done all the children scampered off with merry shouts, only looking back when they had got to a turning in the road and were become breathless. But the man had not moved; and one of the children said, "I'll tell mother, see if I don't"; and another saying, "I wonder if he's a dead man," the others became frightened, and, running on to school, told two men working in a field what they had seen and what they thought; and the men went along to the place where Willie lay, and turned him over and looked on his face.

"Some poor fellow been on the tramp for work, and perished in the storm," the rural constable said when he came to take away the body. They kept it a decent time, but could find out nothing as to its identity. He was not a man, from his clothes, to worry much about. "Found dead," was the verdict of the coroner's jury. And the parish authorities put Willie in an unnamed coffin, and dropped him into a grave

XV

"No, no! You can't see him. It's against the rules. Stand back, Mrs May!"

The words were followed by a faint sound at the entrance to the police-station, as of persons being pushed away: then the voice of Woolven the saddler, saying, "You'd best go home with your daughter, Mrs May, and I'll be company for you part of the way"; and then silence, the noise of the crowd leaving the police-court sounding like a dull confusion afar off, in some world Paul had once visited, but had now left for ever behind. Paul heard with a pained wonder this particular constable speak in so harsh a tone, for he was a man of kindly intention, and had gone beyond his plain duty to show a furtive sympathy with Paul since his imprisonment. But soon it was made obvious that the constable had been playing a part; for two or three minutes later Paul heard him say hurriedly, anxiously:

"Now's your chance, Mrs May! Follow me. Look sharp!—never mind your shawl —he's to be took to Danbridge by the five train. You wait here, Miss May."

There was a hasty movement on the paved corridor before the cells: the door of Paul's cell was thrown open, and the constable, looking in, said in a whisper, "Here's Mrs May wants badly to see you, Penfold. But it's against the rules, so be quick with what you've to say." The constable stood on one side, and Mrs May's frail, dark figure slid into the cell.

She was not weeping: it was commonly believed in Occlesby that she never wept again from the moment she was told of Paul's arrest for the murder of Lord Lusson. Her face, in this grey prison light, expressed a grief that made Paul cry out, "Mrs May! . Mrs May! . . ." And then he said, "I'm so pleased to see you, Mrs May;" and muttered again brokenly, "Mrs May . . . Mrs May . . ."

"Paul," she whispered, ". . . Paul."

"Mrs May," he said, ". . . Mrs May . . ." and pitifully held her hands, that were offered to him shrinkingly from out her faded black shawl. She sighed and shivered at his touch, and seemed afraid to let her eyes meet his.

"Have you heard tidin's of Willie yet, Mrs May?"

"No, Paul——" with a hunted look.

"Nobody thinks——"

"Oh, Paul . . ."

"Mrs May, Mrs May!" he cried, "you must be of good cheer, and Willie'll come back to you and Susan. Ay, ay, Willie's sure to send you his whereabouts when he's found the work he's gone to seek. You'll not grieve so much, Mrs May, as if there was no hope, if you think of that—how Willie's comin home presently, to be with you the same, the breadwinner and comfort to you all." Paul put his face so close to Mrs May's that his beard touched her shoulder. "I've paid much heed to what's been said to the magistrates, and it seems plain that nobody thinks but what him goin' away on the same night was a chance, and there's no sort of suspicion, as I can see, against him. Now, all you've to do, Mrs May," he went on in a low voice, "is to keep silence—not a word to nobody about you comin to see me that night—ay —then Willie'll be restored to you, and he'll be left to work out his repentance before God rather than before man, which is far better. But it depends on you, Mrs May, whether you keep silence or no." He added earnestly, "You can't think of the happiness that's fell on me. I've never known sich a peace. It's what passes understandin."

"Yes, Paul," Mrs May's despairing voice said. "But what casts so deep a trouble on me, Paul, is the thought of my silence—wicked and cruel to the innocent—when I should speak——"

"Ay, I can enter in your feelins, Mrs May, and see it's hard for you to bear. And I've wished since I've been shut up here that I'd known and you not known—so's it would have saved you from the sore trial and conflict of sparin my lonely, useless life, or offerin up the life of your own son—— "

"Paul, Paul, my heart is broke—my heart is broke!"

"No, no, Mrs May," Paul said, and folded the shaking form in his arms. "No, no, Mrs May, it's not come to that, I do hope. And if your heart was to break, Mrs May, be sure Him that's the merciful, and never broke the reed drove to and fro in the wind, would mend it more whole than ever for your bitter trial, and the sake of a mother's love. Mebbe I'm wrong, and I donno what others would say, but I do believe, Mrs May, there's a call far above the law, a order and peacefulness that comes out of tryin to bear one another's burdens, whether our enemies or our friends— ay, it's the way of life, that call, and in my heart I do believe it's been give to you and me."

The constable shuffled his feet: he was standing at some distance from the cell; there were murmurs outside, of people waiting to see the prisoner taken away, waiting to hiss and howl at him. Paul, speaking more cheerfully, said: " " And how's Susan and the children? I hope well. And Lizzie—you've not said how Lizzie is in health, Mrs May. I could hardly bear to look at her when she was givin evidence against me. She did cry bitter, poor lassie."

"Susan's only but poorly, Paul, thank you, and the children is quieter, as if they partly knew what had happened. They was constant askin for you, till their mother stopped them. . . . Oh, Paul, you'll not think no worse of Lizzie for what she's said. She thinks no other but what it's true."

"I could see that," Paul said; "it was plain they all was honest in what they said, and I thought, as I listened to them, was it providential, the network of evidence gatherin round me."

The constable came to the door and said it was time for Mrs May to go. Paul led her out of the cell.

"Now mind you give my love and regard to all at home—and kiss baby and the boys for me—that saucy Jimmy always wipes his cheek when I kiss it—like a boy that, not to be thought a girl. Ay; and tell them I've somethin wonderful, truly very wonderful and rare, for each of them that behaves himself and keeps a good boy while father's away lookin for work—somethin out of my big box they call the Prophet's pawnshop, the impident young rascals. Dearie me, how I've lôved them boys, the more fun they've made of me; I was thinkin of one of Harry's impidences only last night, and had a good laugh to myself. Bless those dear boys!— and their father and mother, and grannie, and Auntie Lizzie. Good-bye, Mrs May."

"Good-bye, Paul."

"Good-bye, Mrs May! And tell Susan whenever she frets, that Willie's sure to be back soon, or send her a long kind letter— and mebbe he'll write to you first, or put a note for you in Susan's letter—and God bless Willie——"

The constable shut the cell door, and hurried Mrs May away. An hour later, Paul, handcuffed, and guarded by four constables, was taken to the county gaol at Danbridge. Woolven the saddler, at the Lusson Arms that night, told the story of the howling of the mob.

XVI

PAUL (so that his spiritual welfare should not be neglected) was taken the next morning before the prison chaplain. The chaplain was seated on a high stool at a desk: he wore eye-glasses, and was writing with a squeaking quill pen in a big book. He glanced over his eye-glasses at Paul, and went on with his writing. He was a Mr Orme, a florid, handsome, obvious man, with good-natured blue eyes, light brown hair (thinning on the crown), and he was shaven so perfectly and was so well groomed that he looked younger than he really was. He was quite orthodox, and quite healthy; his candid friends said he would have made an admirable country gentleman, and the chaplain agreed with them cordially. Paul noticed his splendid shoulders, and thought of Willie May.

"What are you?"

"A Christian," said Paul.

"Oh, but that is rather indefinite."

"No, no," said Paul, "no, no. I'm in a wonder, sir, you should say sich a thing."

This was not said rudely. The chaplain put down his pen, folded his red strong hands (the wrists had a thick coating of yellowish hair), and looked steadily at the prisoner. Then he turned over a page of the book and read something.

"You're name is Penfold?"

"Yes, sir."

"—— Quite so," said the chaplain. He took up his pen again, but did not write. Plainly he was at a loss what to make of this extraordinary person, and as he had not yet been tried, it would hardly have been decorous to preach at him. The chaplain's private admonitions usually ran, "You are a very wicked man, and if you don't repent you'll be damned—in this world and the next." He had used this formula so often that it had come to have almost a humorous sound in his own ears. His conscience had suggested that he should give it up; but then it was so comprehensive, and in most cases so applicable. He felt, however, that something new was needed for the man who stood charged with the murder of Viscount Lusson.

"Is there anything you wish to say to me?"

"Not that I know of, sir."

"I suppose you—feel—rather—lonely——"

"Oh, no, sir; it's very quiet and peaceful here. I felt most lonesome when I was in the exercise yard a bit since. I donno why. Mebbe it was the others that done it."

"What do you mean?"

"They was all so sad and woebegone."

"So they should be! This is a place of sadness." The chaplain tapped on the book, and twirled off his eye-glasses. "People are not here to be happy. They are here because they are wicked, and if they don't repent they will be damned—in this world and the next."

"Ay," said Paul, "ay." He sighed. "But I've thought there's a different way to set about it. I donno that you could make me love God by makin me hate my brother."

"Your brother?" cried the chaplain. "Have you a brother here?"

The chaplain, as Paul looked at him in silence, flushed. A strange, impersonal smile was on Paul's face. He turned his eyes away and gazed out of the window.

"There was men in the yard this mornin," he said, "young men and old, that would have broke down at the sound of one kind word. I saw it in their faces, and I said to myself, if the Lord was to pass by, what would be the power He'd use?"

"The power of love, doubtless," said the chaplain. "But then they would presently crucify Him again."

"Oh—oh—He'd not think the worse of them for that," Paul cried, lifting up his hands, an ecstatic look in his face. "He'd forgive them, and be very, very sorry for them, knowin they was only takin from Him what was of no consequence, and that it would break them down more than ever.

I donno," said Paul, in a softer voice, "how the world's to be subdued except in that way. It's been tryin its own devices long enough, and always it's cryin out, 'Now we're at the door of perfection,' but the door never opens; and if you look into the heart of things, what's been done that was worth doin? I donno, sir, what there can be in human life to seek for, exceptin the wonderful things of love. . . . But I doubt — I doubt I'm keepin you, sir," Paul added, turning aside. He moved a little way round the desk, and pointed out of the window. "Is them pansies yours, sir? I do miss the flowers; and what a comfort it would be to have a cupful of them on my table."

"H'm," coughed the chaplain. "Yes, my man, those are my pansies; but I'm afraid the governor would not allow you to have flowers in your cell." He smiled queerly at the notion. "Still, I don't know; you are an untried prisoner, and I will speak to the governor, if you like."

"No; I wouldn't do that if I was you, sir.

I don't wish to have no difference made in my treatment."

The chaplain screwed up his eyebrows. This was the oddest murderer he had ever had through his hands. He said:

"Your friends, you know, can send in your food."

"Thank you," replied Paul; "but I've no fault to find with the prison fare. It's simple and wholesome, and as good as I've been used to. But I do miss my tea. Poor Mrs May! she could make a nice cup of tea. And the way she brewed it made me that selfish, many a time I've gone and asked her for a cup when I've had tea at home."

"Quite so," said the chaplain. "Now, I must get on with my work. I will come and see you." He thumped on the desk with a ruler, and a warder came in and took Paul away.

The chaplain went every day to Paul's cell to have a chat with the strange being who was so complete a puzzle to him. "They ought to bring him in insane," he said to himself; "but I hardly think they will, in the circumstances. Nor, indeed, would it be easy to prove; and the Judge would make short work of such a defence. And then the poor fellow doesn't seem to care in the least what becomes of him." So Mr Orme, in a spirit of unimaginative inevitableness, settled himself down to the conclusion that in a few weeks he would be called on, in the usual course of legal routine, to read the office for the burial of the dead over Penfold's living body. One day, having wrestled at close quarters with the prisoner, touching the meaning of the words, " I will have mercy, and not sacrifice," the chaplain, who was seated on the edge of the little table in the cell, Paul sitting on the stool, rose on a sudden, and said:

" Well, my man, I shall not come to see you again unless you send for me."

" I hope you will come, sir," Paul said, rising also. " It's very pleasant to hear your voice. You mean so well, and I'd miss your visits."

The chaplain had opened the door; he shut it again, and went back to Paul.

"Tell me, now—this light you are always speaking of—is it a thing that can be seen, and have you seen it?"

"I've seen it," said Paul; "I've seen it."

"Tell me your experience."

"Ah, it's not to be told," Paul said. He seemed to grow suddenly weak, and seated himself again on the stool. "It's one of them experiences," he went on, in a voice so subdued that the chaplain had to bend to hear, "as I should think even the angels only understand imperfect. It's a call and a guidance, and you feel you'll sink if you turn your back on it. I've seen it very clear twice lately——"

"When?" the chaplain incredulously asked.

"I saw it that afternoon in Mrs May's house, when she told me of Lizzie's trouble —ay, and I saw it again the same night, clearer and brighter, in the Little Wood——"

Paul looked up suddenly at the chaplain, and stopped speaking. He set his lips, tried to shake off his abstraction, and his eyes were full of what the chaplain deemed to be terror.

"He was on the point of confessing his guilt," Mr Orme said to himself. He was grown very pale, and went quickly to the door. There he paused, and looked out to see if a warder were near; then turned impulsively, and came back to the prisoner.

"My friend," he said, grasping Paul's hand in a sympathy of which he was afterwards ashamed—"you might have said all this to the stones. But I will not come again. It is better that I should not come—just yet." And the chaplain hastened from the cell.

XVII

So Paul had lonely days before his trial. It depressed him a little, that everyone should seem to take his guilt for granted: yet he would not have had it otherwise.

His cell had a little window high up against the ceiling, with bars across it, though it was so small that he could not have made his escape even had the window been without bars. From this window he could see the changing sky by day, and the purple-black heavens, lighted with stars, by night. And he saw other beautiful things that may not be written down here.

Often he saw Lord Lusson's face as he had seen it that night when the moonlight glorified it in death in the Little Wood; often he saw Willie, and Susan, and their children, and once, baby, whom

Paul, loving all children, loved most, smiled to him, and held out his tiny hands to be taken—all this in the blue and white sky, or in the starlight, Paul saw; and at another time in the night, after his light had been taken away, he saw Willie's baby under great shining wings, baby smiling and crowing, and Willie standing mournful beyond in storm-rent darkness — Willie, who would come back to his wife and little ones, and his careworn mother and friendless sister, when peace had been made with the powers of the world, when human justice had offered up its sacrifice, not to God, but to its own craven, faithless heart, taking the name of the Lord in vain. But Paul's spirit was untouched by bitterness. Once he saw Lizzie, and was very sad because of the darkness that was falling deeper and deeper upon her, and rent his heart at the sight of her sorrowful face, and bowed his head in the loneliness of his cell—and again, looking up at her in his tranced state, his hands just lifted from his knees as he sat on his prison stool, he spoke to her words of comfort, as though her presence were a reality and not the vision of his love. But he never turned away his gaze from the face of Lizzie's mother: no, no; he always smiled as he looked upon her, the sorely afflicted mother, ageing so fast under the load of grief that had fallen on her, under the terrible trial of silence she was enduring for Willie's sake, for Lizzie's sake, for the sake of Susan and the children, for her own sake. Always when he saw her white worn face in his visions, her eyes seemed to have grown unnatural in their absorbed wonder and fixity of mystery, and they were set in a pitiful redness and darkness, but the eyelids never moved, and tears were never seen.

Paul was not a difficult prisoner to manage. He gave no trouble, and made no complaint. The weeks passed, and no one came to see him. He did not murmur at this, remembering how far Danbridge was from Occlesby, and how poor were his friends. It was whispered outside by the warders that he had to be spoken to sometimes two or three times before he understood what was said to him.

One day, however, when the assizes drew near, he was conducted through gloomy corridors and staircases until he found himself in a narrow space with a white wall on one side and a double row of large iron bars on the other. Between the two rows of bars stood a warder; and in another narrow space beyond the farthest row Paul could see two women clutching at the bars and looking through at him with tearful eyes. They were poor women, friends of his in Occlesby, and it had cost them many a hardship to save enough money to pay their railway fares to Danbridge to visit Paul in prison. When the women saw him behind the great iron bars, like a caged beast, they could find no words to say to him: only, "Oh, Paul, Paul!" (said one), and, "Mister Penfold, I never thought as how——" (said the other); and then the women began to cry. They seemed to have really nothing to say to him; and presently, still weeping, they were led away; and they went back to Occlesby, saying, they'd seen the Prophet in gaol, and how happy and contented he looked, but O what a change, so's they'd hardly have known him again for the same man, unless for his eyes, so shiny and pale his face, and his clo'es hangin that slack about his thin body. And after that, no one came to see Paul till the day of his condemnation by the law.

On November—of that year the following paragraph appeared in the newspapers :

"The deformed man, Paul Penfold, who murdered Lord Lusson under circumstances of peculiar brutality, in an unfrequented place known as the Little Wood, near the village of Occlesby, was yesterday, at Danbridge assizes, found guilty of the crime, and duly sentenced to death. There was practically no defence, the accused simply stating when charged that he had nothing to say. He maintained a sullen demeanour throughout the trial. When asked the usual question why sentence should not be passed upon him, the prisoner merely shook his head ; from the first he had shown the utmost indifference to his fate, even closing his eyes and appearing to go to sleep in the dock. The supposition is that he was shamming insanity. He has a crazy appearance, and it was proved that he had all his life been a worthless character. The Judge said he entirely concurred in the verdict, and in passing sentence of death, commented on the heinous nature of the crime, holding out no hope of mercy. At the solemn words, 'And may the Lord have mercy on your soul,' the culprit's lips were seen to move, and he is understood to have muttered 'Amen,' this being the only sign of contrition which he had evinced. A painful sensation was caused in court when his lordship assumed the black cap, an old woman, who had been seated under the gallery, near the dock, rising and calling out hysterically, ' He's innocent! He's innocent!' The Judge sternly ordered her removal, and she was led out of court in a fainting condition. It transpired that she was the mother of the young woman, Elizabeth May, whom the culprit had been courting, and whose intimacy with Lord Lusson was the motive of the murder."

XVIII

So Paul was taken to the cell of the condemned. And the chaplain, visiting him that same night, found him reading the Psalms. He began to read aloud when the chaplain came in.

" List to this, sir ; how you do find things here for every hour. 'The sorrows of death compassed me, and the pains of hell gat hold of me : I found trouble and sorrow. Then called I upon the name of the Lord : O Lord, I beseech thee, deliver my soul. Gracious is the Lord, and righteous; yea, our God is merciful. The Lord preserveth the simple : I was brought low, and He helped me. Return unto thy rest, O my soul' "—Paul raised his voice at these words—" for the Lord hath dealt bountifully with thee. For Thou hast delivered my soul from death, mine eyes from tears, and my feet from fallin———"

But this striking the chaplain as incongruous, he began to speak about the convict's spiritual condition.

"Have you been baptised?"

"I donno," said Paul.

"Then you have not been confirmed?"

"Not how you mean," said Paul, a smile passing over his deep, trustful eyes.

"I think you ought to be baptised and confirmed. The Bishop is a good man; I am sure he would come to the prison for the purpose."

"Ay, you mean well," said Paul, "but I donno it's needful, and I'll not trouble the Bishop. If you see him, he might be willin to say a word for me in his prayers. He's a good man, you say." He added, after a thoughtful silence: "There's a kindness of another sort I'd like to ask you, sir, and it's this. Poor Mrs May is in sad distress—her son Willie bein so long in comin home, and they're all so anxious because he's never sent them a letter to say where he is or what luck he's had—and the kindness, sir, I'd wish you to do, is to sell my hut by the side of the wood at home—I mean Occlesby—and sell also the things that's in it, and take the money to Mrs May, and ask her, if there's a few shillin's to spare, to give them to Susan—that's Willie's wife—to keep the home over her head till Willie comes back. You'll do me this strong favour, sir, I'm sure, after all your kindness in bein so patient with me."

"Yes, willingly, Penfold. But what about yourself? You do not appear to be thinking of yourself at all. You made no defence at your trial, but let things go just anyhow. I am told you would hold no communication with the counsel who was named by the Judge to defend you."

"He did make up a wonderful tale of it out of his head," said Paul, "till I could almost not bear to listen to him, so far he wandered from the truth."

"And now, you know, my dear fellow, you are in a very terrible position."

"For its terribleness, I donno," said Paul. "It's a solemn thing to die, but it's not so dark with me as you'd seem to think, sir. I'm not without comfort. No; I'm not without comfort. What's a man's life, sir—his brief mortal life, that he should be frightened of it bein changed? 'Though He slay me, yet will I love Him.' Mebbe you think the suddenness of it will fright me, but it would always be sudden, in the twinklin of a eye, even if I was to die on my bed, or in a country lane among the flowers, how I've wished it to be, havin a deep yearnin to be quite alone when the change comes. I'd never have thought for the end to come where there's only the eyes of strangers to look on. But it's not for me to decide, and it don't matter except for my own weakness. Oh, Mr Chaplain, there's another point," urged Paul, " in my call on your kindness. I do remember I promised Willie's boys gifts out of my trunk. They'll hold me as a break-promiser if I forget them. It's my trunk what they name, out of their high spirits and warm-hearted ways, the Prophet's pawnshop. Oh dearie me, them boys will miss me, I do believe, and if they was to come in here, you'd see how fond they are of me. There's four of them, one named Paul, after me, though Willie laughed when his dear mother said I might be his godfather, and wouldn't hear tell of it, and besides the four, there's baby, makin five . . . Five little helpless children, and him not come back yet, nor writ a word to say where he is . . . But Willie'll come back——ay, I'll not doubt that; and then the sweet home-nest will be builded up again; and even if he don't, the children won't be forsook, for He always gathers up the lambs in His arms . . . You'll pardon me, sir, owin to my anxious mind; and if you'll take out five little gifts, whatever you think most likely, from my trunk when you go to have the things sold, the choice restin with yourself, and take them to Willie's children, I'll be deep obliged to you."

"I shall do so, certainly, Penfold. But, my dear friend——"

"And please say to each, except to baby, who'd hardly understand at his small time of life, 'This is from Paul's pawnshop, what he promised Grannie May he'd send you, and you must keep them in remembrance of him.' And if also you'd think to tell them, sir, in your own words, how I hold them warm and cosy in my heart, and have put them in my prayers, and always will, and their father and mother and Grannie May and dear Auntie Lizzie—they've always called her Liz, and nobody could break them from it, because they tried, sich is the domineerin way of children —and I donno how you could put it so's not to offend their mother if she was by, but if you could, sir, only a wee word in edgeways, to ask them to try not to think ill of me, when they grow up and understand, mebbe you'd do it, and how thankful I'd be. I'd like you to do it, because it's hard for grown-ups to think well of you, and the good opinion of little children has always been sich a precious thing to me . . ."

The chaplain felt no shame of his tears.

"Penfold," he said in a husky voice, "I can make nothing of you." And presently, in a kind of despair, he left the cell.

Mr Orme made no attempt to dispose of the things in the hut by the wayside. He thought at first that it would be hardly decent to do so at least till after the execution of the criminal. He went, however, to see the place, and found that the poor household gods were of so little value that it would not have been worth while to sell them. They might have been got rid of, to morbid-minded persons, had a fuss been made of the matter; but Mr Orme was a gentleman. So he selected five trifles from Paul's trunk (the place had been ransacked by the police), and locked up the hut. He conveyed the condemned man's message with delicacy and tact; but the mother refused to allow her children to touch the gifts. "He was no relation of ours," said she, "and my husband only let him come here out of pity. I never liked the man." She was flushed and indignant. She cast the things angrily on one side, and Mr Orme had a suspicion that so soon as his back was turned they would be thrown on to the dust heap. He was not altogether out of sympathy with Mrs Willie: though on no account would he have repeated her hard saying to the convict.

The same evening he paid a visit to a rich old lady who had from time to time helped him in the unknown ways of charity. He explained the case in its superficial aspects (which indeed was all he could do), and received a sum of money for Mrs May. The next day he went again to Occlesby, and called at the widow's cottage. She was in bed: her daughter ministering sadly to her needs. The girl did not impress Mr Orme favourably; she was secretive, somewhat morose of manner, and showed a certain reluctance to let the clergyman see her mother. But in his forceful, hearty fashion he made his way into the house, and carried a chair to Mrs May's bedside. She was very weak and depressed, he could see, but apparently was not in pain.

"I'm not really ill, sir; nothing ails me but weakness, and I do believe I'd be better up, in the fresh air. But Lizzie and Susan won't hear of me leavin bed."

"Quite right," said Mr Orme. "Bed, I am sure, is the best place for you, Mrs May."

"Everything's been goin wrong since Willie went away," she murmured. "I do wish he would come home."

Her hands moved incessantly over the counterpane : the feeble thin hands which had interpreted to Paul so much of the pathos of life ; and she kept glancing furtively at the door. Almost every breath was a sigh. As Mr Orme gave her the money he perceived that she was concealing a piece of crumpled newspaper in her hand. Watching her closely, he could not resist the conclusion that she was on the borderland of delirium.

"I'd never have thought" (she said 'sought' like a child) "of it myself. It came to Paul first . . . But Willie will come back in time."

Her mind, he told himself, was "wandering," as Mrs Willie had hinted. The expression of her eyes impressed him painfully.

"Oh, you must look on the bright side of things, Mrs May. You have many kind friends, you know. And I hope you will soon be strong enough to be up and about as usual."

"Never again," she said. "It's my death-blow; I feel it on me. But I'd never have thought of it myself. It came to Paul first."

Mr Orme did not prolong his stay.

"You must do as your daughter tells you," he said, putting aside his chair.

"But she makes me keep in bed, and I want to see the Queen. She's a good woman, and has sons of her own, and if I was to tell her private, I'm sure she'd have pity on me, and on Willie and Paul, and all of us. Them others don't know a mother's heart and the cost of the word that should be spoke, but if I could find the Queen and tell her in secret, she'd know how to mend our troubles. I'd write to her, only I don't know where she is, and the others might open it. I was dreamin all last night that she came in here, and sat by my bed, O sich a kind face, and I told her, and she took my hand and I saw the tears in her eyes—and when I said to her, 'Dear Queen, Paul thought of it first, not me,' she said, 'I'll make him a hero in my kingdom'——"

"Quite so, quite so," said Mr Orme.

Lizzie followed the clergyman, when he was leaving, to the outer door.

"I noticed," he said, "that your mother was holding a piece of paper in her hand. She appeared to be desirous that I should not see it. Do you know that she has it?"

"Yes, sir; it's a scrap she tore out of a newspaper a neighbour brought in—the place where it gives the day and hour when Paul Penfold is to be . . . hanged in Danbridge gaol," Lizzie breathed, holding down her head.

"What is she doing with it?"

"I can't think. She was very fond of him."

"So I should say. His dreadful position seems to be preying on her mind. You ought to get the piece of paper from her, and try to make her forget it."

"I've tried, sir, but I can't make her give it up. And she's always begging me to let her put on her clothes and go and look for my brother. Last night I found her out of bed and made her go back. She said she wanted to see the Queen. It's her mind, sir."

"Yes, of course; and you must take great care of her. I am very, very sorry," said the chaplain. "Penfold wishes that you should have his things. But I think it would be more seemly to leave them where they are till later. Here is the key."

"I don't want it," said Lizzie, turning away. "We'd not touch his things. We've not sunk as low as that."

"Very well," said Mr Orme; "I will keep the key for the present." He added, as he shook hands with the trembling girl, "You must keep a constant watch on your poor mother. There is no saying what she might do in her delirious condition. I will send a doctor from Danbridge, and will call again in a day or two to see how she is getting on."

XIX

A NIGHT of vehement stars and remote silences: a surreptitious sullen dawn: then angry skies, and a bitter northern wind sweeping down on Danbridge gaol. Only a few persons had come forth on this bleak November morning to see the black flag that should tell of the strangling of Paul Penfold; others, in the town, would see it from their windows at breakfast-time. The people were gathered in twos and threes, in large groups, and in shame-faced singles, on the broad road in front of the gaol, and Woolven the saddler and Andrew Isted were of them. Woolven had never seen a black flag go up, and being an old man, this might be his last chance; and Andrew Isted had never missed one these twenty years, and told gruesome tales at the Lusson Arms. So they had borrowed a vehicle and driven out from Occlesby; and it was with pained surprise that they discovered that Mrs May had got to Danbridge gaol before them.

"Poor old woman, it's a grievous thing to see her here, so wore out and forlorn," said the saddler. "I'd not marvel but she's made her escape from home in despite of her daughter's care of her. See her there, Andrew, scarce fit to stand. Bless my soul, from her muddy draggled clothes she must have been walkin through the whole night to be here in time."

"It's a funny taste in a woman," Andrew Isted said, "to want to see the black flag hoist—for the man she was fond of, too. She must be out of her mind. I've heard rumours."

"So've I. What a wreck she is!"

"I'm willin to go along to that public," said Andrew, "and fetch a drop of something to put a bit of life in her. She's more dead than alive, from her appearance."

"Best wait till it's over; then we'll take her back home in the trap," said Woolven. "I do declare she's got a bunch of winter what-d'ye-call-'em — daisies — in her hand. She must have gathered them in her son's garden, for there's none in her own. They look as if they'd been down in the slush."

"So she does the same," said Andrew.

Woolven looked at his watch.

"What d'ye make the right hour to be, Andrew? The trap joltin' has stopped mine."

"Seven to eight."

"Late's that? Eh, time do fly—though I expect it's shorter over there than on this side, where life is in our own hands, so to to speak. You're sure it's to be done at eight?"

"Eight sharp; that's the fixed constitutional hour, and they couldn't alter it except from Act of Parliament."

"I've no doubt," said Woolven the saddler, "but what it's held at one set hour to force the nation to think of it all at once. It's a horrible wide impression, and in one way it ought to make the hanged man feel he's plenty of company, though I hardly suppose it does, seein the state of mind he's in."

"The bell's been tollin for ten minutes or more," said Andrew. "He'll hear it in his cell."

"Sure enough to. They say he's as quiet as a mouse, nearly always smilin—he did have a sweet sort of smile, I must say, for a man of his class—and what's more strange, I've heard his deformity's left him, and he walks now with a real gentleman-like, noble air. I can't speak for the truth of it, though it might be proved on the ground of miracle, a thing not likely to happen in a gaol. But what a state to be in, to sit listening to your own funeral knell, then to hear the parson read the Prayer Book over you, like they do when the coffin is lowered. I do believe," said the saddler, "it was the closin of the rhododendron walk that made the last turn in his senses. I've never felt confident in my own mind he done it out of jealousy for Lizzie. No, no; he was touched up here, from his mad notions of justice, if ever a man was. It's been comin on him too; why, I do remember he never could tell the right day of the week, whether the first, middle, or end, and Sundays only came upon him by instinct, like boys for the time of marbles and kites. . . . Andrew, that bell do make me feel bad. What's the hour by your watch now, lad?"

"Four to eight." Andrew held his watch in his hand.

A profound awe had settled upon the watchers; few words were spoken, and these in whispers. Certain women stood afar off on the road where it wound into the town. Only one woman was near; a woman unsexed by sorrow; a woman who had been a living prayer since these sad things began. She stood before the great barred gates of the prison, holding up her handful of winter daisies, as if this were her last peace-offering. Her head was bare, and her thin white hair was matted with rain. The ends of her black shawl blew in the wind, like the signals of a broken heart, in a world that had eyes to see and saw not, and ears to hear and heard not. None saw her face now, so near she was to the gates. None heard her anguished supplication: " If only Willie would come back. .

Paul, Paul. . . . Paul, Paul. . . . I donno what to do. . . ." And the bell tolled, tolled ; and the last minutes fled ; and Paul was handed over to the common hangman. . . .

A little child, its face and arms blue from the cold, came up on the broad road, and Woolven the saddler gave it a penny and sent it home. The women farther down called it to them, and hid it among them. A couple of young fellows, pulsing with the greed of life, got close to the high bare wall, and listened.

"The scaffold's just over there," said one. "I've seen it—only a thing like a big well. You'd never know unless you was told. Two posts, and a bar across. He stands under the bar on two folding doors, and when the doors open down he goes, and then his head'll be on a level where we're standing. I wish there was a hole in this wall!"

"So do I. He's as good as dead by now, from fright, I daresay," said the other.

"No ; they say he's rather game."

"Andrew, lad," Woolven whispered, "what's the clock now?"

"Half a minute——"

"Andrew, I'll take your arm; I doubt I m goin to be took ill. I do wish I'd never come."

"Ssh!" Andrew said. "There's a voice——"

"What d'ye hear, Andrew?"

"Only the voice. Like prayer. Haah!— hear that? — The Lord have mercy on him!——"

The voice on the other side of the wall ceased. Another was vaguely audible, flung on the screaming wind. The black flag swished and bleated over the prison gates. Woolven took off his hat, and for a moment looked down to the ground. Andrew Isted cleared his throat, and turned away his eyes. The young men by the wall ran out into the middle of the road to look at the flag.

"Well, to be sure, a queer world," said Andrew Isted, sighing. "Who'd have thought this would be the end of Prophet Penfold?"

Woolven wiped his eyes with a red handkerchief, caring not who should see him in this weakness. "Nobody, lad, nobody. Not one that knew Paul would ever have dreamt it! I almost feel as if another murder had been done—it's a kind of presentiment here;" he put his hand on his heart. "If it's not a profane thought, Andrew," he added, gazing upward, "I wonder what God is sayin to Paul now?——"

"Ah, that's a puzzler," said Andrew. "But there's Mrs May gone right up to the gate. What's she waiting for, I wonder?"

"She don't seem to understand he's come to his end," said Woolven. "What a heartbreakin look she has. I'll go and ask her to come away in our trap; we'll make room for her among the straw, where she'll get a rest, and there's a rug to put over her. Why, she's knockin at the gate. Andrew! she's fell on her knees——"

The little gate set in the greater gate was opened from within, and the chaplain stepped sadly forth into the freer air. His eyes were red, and he seemed to have lost his self-command. He uttered an exclamation, and raised the widow from the ground.

"Mrs May, Mrs May—you should not be here on such a morning!"

She gazed at him in stony hopelessness, and held out her bunch of winter daisies.

"I'm looking for my boy Willie. I've walked from Occlesby seekin him, in the night for fear Lizzie'd find out I left my bed. She don't know—nobody knows but me. I can't go home till I've found my Willie."

"Oh, you will find him—of course," the chaplain said kindly; scarce knowing what to say.

He kept his arm about her: she was become too exhausted to stand alone. She rubbed her frozen hand up and down his sleeve; then placing her daisies upon his broad chest, held her head on one side in a child-like way to see the effect, and began to laugh wonderfully.

"It was Paul thought of it first," she said; "I'd never have thought of it myself. I'm that troubled in my mind, sir. . . . You're his true friend, and if you'll give him these flowers, from Willie's garden. . . . Oh, if only I could see the Queen. . . . But Willie'll set everything to rights when he comes home. He was always sich a good son to his mother, as never was. . . ."

THE END

1896.

List of Books
IN
BELLES LETTRES
(Including some Transfers)
Published by John Lane
The Bodley Head
VIGO STREET, LONDON, W.

ADAMS (FRANCIS).
    ESSAYS IN MODERNITY. Crown 8vo. 5s. net. [*Shortly.*
        Chicago: Stone & Kimball.
    A CHILD OF THE AGE. (*See* KEYNOTES SERIES.)
ALDRICH (T. B.).
    LATER LYRICS. Sm. fcap. 8vo, 2s. 6d. net.
        Boston and New York: Houghton, Mifflin & Co.
ALLEN (GRANT).
    THE LOWER SLOPES: A Volume of Verse. With Title-page and Cover Design by J. ILLINGWORTH KAY. Crown 8vo. 5s. net.
        Chicago: Stone & Kimball.
    THE WOMAN WHO DID. (*See* KEYNOTES SERIES.)
    THE BRITISH BARBARIANS. (*See* KEYNOTES SERIES.)
ARCADY LIBRARY (THE).
    A SERIES OF OPEN-AIR BOOKS. Edited by J. S. FLETCHER. With cover designs by PATTEN WILSON. Cr 8vo. 5s. net.
        Vol. I. ROUND ABOUT A BRIGHTON COACH OFFICE. By MAUDE EGERTON KING. With over 30 illustrations by LUCY KEMP-WELCH.
        The following are in preparation.
        Vol. II. SCHOLAR GIPSIES. By JOHN BUCHAN. With seven full-page etchings by D. Y. CAMERON.
        Vol. III. LIFE IN ARCADIA. By J. S. FLETCHER. Illustrated by PATTEN WILSON.
        Vol. IV. A GARDEN OF PEACE. By HELEN CROFTON With illustrations by EDMUND H. NEW.
        New York: Macmillan & Co.

BEECHING (REV. H. C.).
  IN A GARDEN: Poems. With Title-page designed by
    ROGER FRY. Crown 8vo. 5s. net.
    New York: Macmillan & Co.
BEERBOHM (MAX).
  THE WORKS OF MAX BEERBOHM. With a Bibliography
    by JOHN LANE. Sq. 16mo. 4s. 6d. net.
    New York: Charles Scribner's Sons.
BENSON (ARTHUR CHRISTOPHER).
  LYRICS. Fcap. 8vo, buckram. 5s. net.
    New York: Macmillan & Co.
BODLEY HEAD ANTHOLOGIES (THE).
  Edited by ROBERT H. CASE. With title-page and cover
    designs by WALTER WEST. Each Volume cr. 8vo.
    5s. net.
  Vol. I. ENGLISH EPITHALAMIES. by ROBERT H. CASE.
  Vol. II. MUSA PISCATRIX. By JOHN BUCHAN. With
    six etchings by E. PHILIP PIMLOTT.
  Vol. III. ENGLISH ELEGIES. By JOHN C. BAILEY.
  Vol. IV. ENGLISH SATIRES. By CHARLES HILL DICK.
BRIDGES (ROBERT).
  SUPPRESSED CHAPTERS AND OTHER BOOKISHNESS.
    Crown 8vo. 3s. 6d. net.   [*Second Edition*.
    New York: Charles Scribner's Sons.
BROTHERTON (MARY).
  ROSEMARY FOR REMEMBRANCE. With Title-page and Cover
    Design by WALTER WEST. Fcap. 8vo. 3s. 6d. net.
CRANE (WALTER).
  TOY BOOKS. Re-issue. Each with new Cover Design and
    end papers. 9d. net.
    I. THIS LITTLE PIG.
    II. THE FAIRY SHIP.
    III. KING LUCKIEBOY'S PARTY.
  The group of three bound in one volume, with a decorative cloth cover, end papers, and a newly written and designed title-page and preface. 3s. 6d. net.
    Chicago: Stone & Kimball.
DALMON (C. W.).
  SONG FAVOURS. With a Title-page designed by J. P.
    DONNE. Sq. 16mo. 3s. 6d. net.
    Chicago: Way & Williams.

DAVIDSON (JOHN).

PLAYS: An Unhistorical Pastoral; A Romantic Farce; Bruce, a Chronicle Play; Smith, a Tragic Farce; Scaramouch in Naxos, a Pantomime, with a Frontispiece and Cover Design by AUBREY BEARDSLEY. Small 4to. 7s. 6d. net.
Chicago: Stone & Kimball.

FLEET STREET ECLOGUES. Fcap. 8vo, buckram. 4s. 6d. net. [*Third Edition.*

FLEET STREET ECLOGUES. 2nd Series. Fcap. 8vo, buckram. 4s. 6d. net. [*Second Edition.*
New York: Dodd, Mead & Co.

A RANDOM ITINERARY AND A BALLAD. With a Frontispiece and Title-page by LAURENCE HOUSMAN. 600 copies. Fcap. 8vo, Irish Linen. 5s. net.
Boston: Copeland & Day.

BALLADS AND SONGS. With a Title-page and Cover Design by WALTER WEST. Fcap. 8vo, buckram. 5s. net. [*Fourth Edition.*
Boston: Copeland & Day.

DE TABLEY (LORD).

POEMS, DRAMATIC AND LYRICAL. By JOHN LEICESTER WARREN (Lord De Tabley). Illustrations and Cover Design by C. S. RICKETTS. Crown 8vo. 7s. 6d. net. [*Third Edition.*

POEMS, DRAMATIC AND LYRICAL. Second Series, uniform in binding with the former volume. Crown 8vo. 5s. net.
New York: Macmillan & Co.

EGERTON (GEORGE).

KEYNOTES. (*See* KEYNOTES SERIES.)
DISCORDS. (*See* KEYNOTES SERIES.)
YOUNG OFEG'S DITTIES. A translation from the Swedish of OLA HANSSON. With Title-page and Cover Design by AUBREY BEARDSLEY. Crown 8vo. 3s. 6d. net.
Boston: Roberts Bros.

EVE'S LIBRARY.

Each volume crown 8vo. 3s. 6d. net.
Vol. I. SIX MODERN WOMEN: an English Rendering of LAURA MARHOLM HANSSON'S 'DAS BUCH DER FRAUEN.' By HERMIONE RAMSDEN. Subjects dealt with:—Sonia Kovalevsky; George Egerton; Eleonora Duse; Amalie Skram; Marie Bashkersteff; A. Ch. Edgren-Leffler.

EVE'S LIBRARY—*continued.*
    Vol. II. THE ASCENT OF WOMAN. By Mrs ROY DEVEREUX.
    Vol. III. MARRIAGE QUESTIONS IN MODERN FICTION. By E. R. CHAPMAN.

FIELD (EUGENE).
    THE LOVE AFFAIRS OF A BIBLIOMANIAC. Post 8vo. 3s. 6d. net.
        New York : Charles Scribner's Sons.

FLETCHER (J. S.).
    THE WONDERFUL WAPENTAKE. By 'A SON OF THE SOIL.' With 18 full-page Illustrations by J. A. SYMINGTON. Crown 8vo. 5s. 6d. net.
        Chicago : A. C. McClurg & Co.
    LIFE IN ARCADIA. (*See* ARCADY LIBRARY.)

FOUR AND SIX-PENNY NOVELS.
    Each Volume with title-page and cover design by PATTEN WILSON. Crown 8vo. 4s. 6d. net.
    GALLOPING DICK. By H. B. MARRIOTT WATSON.
        New York : The Frederick A. Stokes Co.
    THE WOOD OF THE BRAMBLES. By FRANK MATHEW.
        Chicago : Way & Williams.
    THE SACRIFICE OF FOOLS. By R. MANIFOLD CRAIG.
        Chicago : Stone & Kimball.

        The following are in preparation.
    A LAWYER'S WIFE. By SIR NEVILL GEARY, BART.
    WEIGHED IN THE BALANCE. By HARRY LANDER.
    GLAMOUR. By META ORRED.
    PATIENCE SPARHAWK AND HER TIMES. By GERTRUDE ATHERTON.
    THE CAREER OF DELIA HASTINGS. By H. B. MARRIOTT WATSON.

GALE (NORMAN).
    ORCHARD SONGS. With Title-page and Cover Design by J. ILLINGWORTH KAY. Fcap. 8vo, Irish Linen. 5s. net.
        Also a Special Edition limited in number on hand-made paper bound in English vellum. £1, 1s. net.
        New York : G. P. Putnam's Sons.

GARNETT (RICHARD).
    POEMS. With Title-page by J. ILLINGWORTH KAY. Crown 8vo. 5s. net.
    DANTE, PETRARCH, CAMOENS, cxxiv Sonnets rendered in English. Crown 8vo. 5s. net.
        Boston: Copeland & Day.

GIBSON (CHARLES DANA).
    PICTURES: Nearly One Hundred Large Cartoons. Oblong Folio. 15s. net.
        New York: R. H. Russell & Son.

GOSSE (EDMUND).
    THE LETTERS OF THOMAS LOVELL BEDDOES. Now first edited. Pott 8vo. 5s. net.
        Also 25 copies large paper. 12s. 6d. net.
        New York: Macmillan & Co.

GRAHAME (KENNETH).
    PAGAN PAPERS: A Volume of Essays. With Title-page by AUBREY BEARDSLEY. Fcap. 8vo. 5s. net.
        [*Out of print at present.*
    THE GOLDEN AGE. Crown 8vo. 3s. 6d. net.
        [*Third Edition.*
        Chicago: Stone & Kimball.

GREENE (G. A.).
    ITALIAN LYRISTS OF TO-DAY. Translations in the original metres from about thirty-five living Italian poets, with bibliographical and biographical notes. Crown 8vo. 5s. net.
        New York: Macmillan & Co.

GREENWOOD (FREDERICK).
    IMAGINATION IN DREAMS. Crown 8vo. 5s. net.
        New York: Macmillan & Co.

HAKE (T. GORDON).
    A SELECTION FROM HIS POEMS. Edited by Mrs MEYNELL. With a Portrait after D. G. ROSSETTI, and a Cover Design by GLEESON WHITE. Crown 8vo. 5s. net.
        Chicago: Stone and Kimball.

HAYES (ALFRED).
    THE VALE OF ARDEN AND OTHER POEMS. With a Title-page and a Cover designed by E. H. NEW. Fcap. 8vo. 3s. 6d. net.
        Also 25 copies large paper. 15s. net.

HAZLITT (WILLIAM).
  LIBER AMORIS, OR THE NEW PYGMALION. A New
  Edition from the Original MS. With Letters and a
  Diary never before printed. Portrait after BEWICK,
  and Facsimiles, and a lengthy Introduction by
  RICHARD LE GALLIENNE. 4to, buckram. 21s. net.
HEINEMANN (WILLIAM).
  THE FIRST STEP. A Dramatic Moment. Small 4to.
  3s. 6d. net.
HOPPER (NORA).
  BALLADS IN PROSE. With a Title-page and Cover by
  WALTER WEST. Sq. 16mo. 5s. net.
    Boston: Roberts Bros.
  UNDER QUICKEN BOUGHS. With Title-page designed by
  PATTEN WILSON. Cr. 8vo. 5s. net.
HOUSMAN (CLEMENCE).
  THE WERE WOLF. With six Full-page Illustrations,
  Title-page and Cover Design, by LAURENCE HOUS-
  MAN. Sq. 16mo. 3s. 6d. net.
    Chicago: Way & Williams.
HOUSMAN (LAURENCE).
  GREEN ARRAS: Poems. With Illustrations by the
  Author. Crown 8vo. 5s. net. [*In preparation.*
IRVING (LAURENCE).
  GODEFROI AND YOLANDE: A Play. Sm. 4to. 3s. 6d.
  net. [*In preparation.*
JAMES (W. P.).
  ROMANTIC PROFESSIONS: A Volume of Essays. With
  Title - page designed by J. ILLINGWORTH KAY.
  Crown 8vo. 5s. net.
    New York: Macmillan & Co.
JOHNSON (LIONEL).
  THE ART OF THOMAS HARDY: Six Essays. With Etched
  Portrait by WM. STRANG, and Bibliography by JOHN
  LANE. Crown 8vo. 5s. 6d. net. [*Second Edition.*
    Also 150 copies, large paper, with proofs of the portrait. £1, 1s.
  net.
    New York: Dodd, Mead & Co.
JOHNSON (PAULINE).
  WHITE WAMPUM: Poems. With a Title-page and Cover
  Design by E. H. NEW. Crown 8vo. 5s. net.
    Boston: Lamson, Wolffe & Co.

JOHNSTONE (C. E.).
BALLADS OF BOY AND BEAK. With a Title-page designed by F. H. TOWNSEND. Sq. 32mo. 2s. net.

KEYNOTES SERIES.
Each volume with specially designed Title-page by AUBREY BEARDSLEY. Crown 8vo, cloth. 3s. 6d. net.

Vol. I. KEYNOTES. By GEORGE EGERTON.
[*Seventh edition.*

Vol. II. THE DANCING FAUN. By FLORENCE FARR.

Vol. III. POOR FOLK. Translated from the Russian of F. Dostoievsky by LENA MILMAN. With a Preface by GEORGE MOORE.

Vol. IV. A CHILD OF THE AGE. By FRANCIS ADAMS.

Vol. V. THE GREAT GOD PAN AND THE INMOST LIGHT. By ARTHUR MACHEN. [*Second edition.*

Vol. VI. DISCORDS. By GEORGE EGERTON.
[*Fourth edition.*

Vol. VII. PRINCE ZALESKI. By M. P. SHIEL.

Vol. VIII. THE WOMAN WHO DID. By GRANT ALLEN.
[*Twenty-second edition.*

Vol. IX. WOMEN'S TRAGEDIES. By H. D. LOWRY.

Vol. X. GREY ROSES. By HENRY HARLAND.

Vol. XI. AT THE FIRST CORNER AND OTHER STORIES. By H. B. MARRIOTT WATSON.

Vol. XII. MONOCHROMES. By ELLA D'ARCY.

Vol. XIII. AT THE RELTON ARMS. By EVELYN SHARP.

Vol. XIV. THE GIRL FROM THE FARM. By GERTRUDE DIX. [*Second edition.*

Vol. XV. THE MIRROR OF MUSIC. By STANLEY V. MAKOWER.

Vol. XVI. YELLOW AND WHITE. By W. CARLTON DAWE.

Vol. XVII. THE MOUNTAIN LOVERS. By FIONA MACLEOD.

Vol. XVIII. THE WOMAN WHO DIDN'T. By VICTORIA CROSSE. [*Third edition.*

Vol. XIX. THE THREE IMPOSTORS. By ARTHUR MACHEN.

Vol. XX. NOBODY'S FAULT. By NETTA SYRETT.

KEYNOTES SERIES—*continued.*
   Vol. XXI. THE BRITISH BARBARIANS. By GRANT ALLEN.
                                                          [*Second edition.*
   Vol. XXII. IN HOMESPUN. By E. NESBIT.
   Vol. XXIII. PLATONIC AFFECTIONS. By JOHN SMITH.
   Vol. XXIV. NETS FOR THE WIND. By UNA TAYLOR.
   Vol. XXV. WHERE THE ATLANTIC MEETS THE LAND.
     By CALDWELL LIPSETT.

     The following are in rapid preparation.

   Vol. XXVI. IN SCARLET AND GREY. By the Hon. MRS
     ARTHUR HENNIKER. (With a story, 'The Spectre
     of the Real,' written in collaboration with THOMAS
     HARDY.
   Vol. XXVIII. MARIS STELLA. By MARIE CLOTHILDE
     BALFOUR.
   Vol. XXVIII. MORRISON'S HEIR. By MABEL E. WOTTON.
   Vol. XXIX. SHAPES IN THE FIRE. By M. P. SHIEL.
   Vol. XXX. UGLY IDOL. By CLAUDE NICHOLSON.
     Boston : Roberts Bros.

LANE'S LIBRARY.
        Each volume Cr. 8vo. 3s. 6d. net.
   Vol. I. MARCH HARES. By GEORGE FORTH.
   Vol. II. THE SENTIMENTAL SEX. By GERTRUDE WAR-
     DEN.
   Vol. III. GOLD. By ANNIE LUDEN.
   Vol. IV. THE SENTIMENTAL VIKINGS. By R. V. RISLEY.

LEATHER (R. K.).
   VERSES. 250 copies. Fcap. 8vo. 3s. net.
     Transferred by the Author to the present Publisher.

LE GALLIENNE (RICHARD).
   PROSE FANCIES. With Portrait of the Author by
     WILSON STEER. Fourth Edition. Crown 8vo.
     Purple cloth. 5s. net.
       Also a limited large paper edition. 12s. 6d. net.
     New York : G. P. Putnam's Sons.
   THE BOOK BILLS OF NARCISSUS, An Account rendered
     by RICHARD LE GALLIENNE. Third Edition. With
     a Frontispiece. Crown 8vo. Purple cloth. 3s. 6d. net.
       Also 50 copies on large paper. 8vo. 10s. 6d. net.
     New York : G. P. Putman's Sons.

LE GALLIENNE (RICHARD)—*continued.*

> ROBERT LOUIS STEVENSON, AN ELEGY, AND OTHER POEMS, MAINLY PERSONAL. With Etched Title-page by D. Y. CAMERON. Cr. 8vo. Purple cloth. 4s. 6d. net.
> Also 75 copies on large paper. 8vo. 12s. 6d. net.
>> Boston: Copeland & Day.
>
> ENGLISH POEMS. Fourth Edition, revised. Crown 8vo. Purple cloth. 4s. 6d. net.
>> Boston: Copeland & Day.
>
> RETROSPECTIVE REVIEWS, A LITERARY LOG, 1891-1895. 2 vols. crown 8vo. Purple cloth. 9s. net.
>> New York: Dodd, Mead & Co.
>
> GEORGE MEREDITH: Some Characteristics. With a Bibliography (much enlarged) by JOHN LANE, Portrait, etc. Fourth Edition. Cr. 8vo. Purple cloth. 5s. 6d. net.
>
> THE RELIGION OF A LITERARY MAN. 5th thousand. Crown 8vo. Purple cloth. 3s. 6d. net.
> Also a special rubricated edition on hand-made paper. 8vo. 10s. 6d. net.
>> New York: G. P. Putnam's Sons.
>
> PROSE FANCIES. Second Series. Cr. 8vo, purple cloth. 5s. net.   [*In preparation.*
>
> See also HAZLITT.

LUCAS (WINIFRED).
> A VOLUME OF POEMS. Fcap. 8vo. 4s. 6d. net.
> [*In preparation.*

LYNCH (HANNAH).
> THE GREAT GALEOTO AND FOLLY OR SAINTLINESS. Two Plays, from the Spanish of JOSÉ ECHEGARAY, with an Introduction. Small 4to. 5s. 6d. net.
>> Boston: Lamson, Wolffe & Co.

MARZIALS (THEO.).
> THE GALLERY OF PIGEONS AND OTHER POEMS. Post 8vo. 4s. 6d. net.   [*Very few remain.*
> *Transferred by the Author to the present Publisher.*

THE MAYFAIR SET.
> Each volume fcap. 8vo. 3s. 6d. net.
>> Vol. I. THE AUTOBIOGRAPHY OF A BOY: Passages selected by his Friend, G. S. STREET. With Title-page by C. W. FURSE.   [*Fifth Edition.*

THE MAYFAIR SET—*continued*.
>   Vol. II. THE JONESES AND THE ASTERISKS: a Story in Monologue. By GERALD CAMPBELL. With Title-page and six Illustrations by F. H. TOWNSEND.
>   [*Second Edition*.
>   Vol. III. SELECT CONVERSATIONS WITH AN UNCLE NOW EXTINCT. By H. G. WELLS. With Title-page by F. H. TOWNSEND.
>   Vol. IV. FOR PLAIN WOMEN ONLY. By GEORGE FLEMING. With Title-page by PATTEN WILSON.
>   Vol. V. THE FEASTS OF AUTOLYCUS: The Diary of a Greedy Woman. Edited by ELIZABETH ROBINS PENNELL. With Title-page by PATTEN WILSON.
>   Vol. VI. MRS ALBERT GRUNDY: Observations in Philistia. By HAROLD FREDERIC. With Title-page by PATTEN WILSON.
>   New York: The Merriam Company.

MEREDITH (GEORGE).
>   THE FIRST PUBLISHED PORTRAIT OF THIS AUTHOR, engraved on the wood by W. BISCOMBE GARDNER, after the painting by G. F. WATTS. Proof copies on Japanese vellum, signed by painter and engraver. £1, 1s. net.

MEYNELL (MRS), (ALICE C. THOMPSON).
>   POEMS. Fcap. 8vo. 3s. 6d. net. [*Third Edition*.
>   A few of the 50 large paper copies (First Edition) remain, 12s. 6d. net.
>   THE RHYTHM OF LIFE AND OTHER ESSAYS. Fcap 8vo. 3s. 6d. net. [*Third Edition*.
>   A few of the 50 large paper copies (First Edition) remain, 12s. 6d. net.
>   THE COLOUR OF LIFE AND OTHER ESSAYS. Fcap. 8vo. 3s. 6d. net. [*In preparation*.
>   *See also* HAKE.

MILLER (JOAQUIN).
>   THE BUILDING OF THE CITY BEAUTIFUL. Fcap. 8vo. With a Decorated Cover. 5s. net.
>   Chicago: Stone & Kimball.

MONKHOUSE (ALLAN).
>   BOOKS AND PLAYS: A Volume of Essays on Meredith, Borrow, Ibsen, and others. Crown 8vo. 5s. net.
>   Philadelphia: J. B. Lippincott Co.

NESBIT (E.).
> A POMANDER OF VERSE. With a Title-page and Cover designed by LAURENCE HOUSMAN. Crown 8vo. 5s. net.
>> Chicago: A. C. McClurg & Co.
> IN HOMESPUN. (*See* KEYNOTES SERIES.)

NETTLESHIP (J. T.).
> ROBERT BROWNING: Essays and Thoughts. With a Portrait. Crown 8vo. 5s. 6d. net. [*Third Edition*.
>> New York: Chas. Scribner's Sons.

NOBLE (JAS. ASHCROFT).
> THE SONNET IN ENGLAND AND OTHER ESSAYS. Title-page and Cover Design by AUSTIN YOUNG. Crown 8vo. 5s. net.
>> Also 50 copies large paper. 12s. 6d. net.

O'SHAUGHNESSY (ARTHUR).
> HIS LIFE AND HIS WORK. With Selections from his Poems. By LOUISE CHANDLER MOULTON. Portrait and Cover Design. Fcap. 8vo. 5s. net.
>> Chicago: Stone & Kimball.

OXFORD CHARACTERS.
> A series of 24 portraits by WILL ROTHENSTEIN, with text by F. YORK POWELL and others. 200 copies only, folio, buckram, £3, 3s. net.
> 25 special large paper copies containing proof impressions of the portraits signed by the artist, £6, 6s. net.

PETERS (WM. THEODORE).
> POSIES OUT OF RINGS. With Title-page by PATTEN WILSON. Sq. 16mo. 2s. net.
>> [*In preparation.*

PIERROT'S LIBRARY.
> Each volume with Title-page, Cover Design, and End-papers designed by AUBREY BEARDSLEY. Sq. 16mo. 2s. net.
>> Vol. I. PIERROT. By H. DE VERE STACPOOLE.
>> Vol. II. MY LITTLE LADY ANNE. By Mrs EGERTON CASTLE.
>> Vol. III. SIMPLICITY. By A. T. G. PRICE.
>> Vol. IV. MY BROTHER. By VINCENT BROWN.

PIERROT'S LIBRARY—*continued*.
  Vol. v. DEATH, THE KNIGHT AND THE LADY. By
    H. DE VERE STACPOOLE. [*In preparation.*
PLARR (VICTOR).
  IN THE DORIAN MOOD: Poems. With a Title-page by
    PATTEN WILSON. Crown 8vo. 5s. net.
      [*In preparation.*
RADFORD (DOLLIE).
  SONGS AND OTHER VERSES. With Title-page designed
    by PATTEN WILSON. Fcap. 8vo. 4s. 6d. net.
    Philadelphia: J. B. Lippincott Co.
RHYS (ERNEST).
  A LONDON ROSE AND OTHER RHYMES. With Title-page
    designed by SELWYN IMAGE. Crown 8vo. 5s. net.
    New York: Dodd, Mead & Co.
RICKETTS (C. S.) AND C. H. SHANNON.
  HERO AND LEANDER. By CHRISTOPHER MARLOWE
    and GEORGE CHAPMAN. With Borders, Initials, and
    Illustrations designed and engraved on the wood by
    C. S. RICKETTS and C. H. SHANNON. Bound in
    English vellum and gold. 200 copies only. 35s. net.
    Boston: Copeland & Day.
ROBERTSON (JOHN M.).
  ESSAYS TOWARDS A CRITICAL METHOD. (New Series.)
    Crown 8vo. 5s. net. [*In preparation.*
ST CYRES (LORD).
  THE LITTLE FLOWERS OF ST FRANCIS: A new ren-
    dering into English of the Fioretti di San Francesco.
    Crown 8vo. 5s. net. [*In preparation.*
SHORE (LOUISA).
  POEMS. With a Memoir by FREDERICK HARRISON.
    Fcap. 8vo. 5s. net. [*In preparation.*
STEVENSON (ROBERT LOUIS).
  PRINCE OTTO. A rendering in French by EGERTON
    CASTLE. With frontispiece, title-page, and cover
    designs by D. Y. Cameron. Crown 8vo. 7s. 6d net.
      [*In preparation.*
    Also 100 copies on large paper, uniform in size with the Edinburgh
    Edition of the Works.

  A CHILD'S GARDEN OF VERSES. With over 150 Illustra-
    tions by CHARLES ROBINSON. Crown 8vo. 5s. net.
      [*Second Edition.*

STODDART (THOS. TOD).
> THE DEATH WAKE. With an Introduction by ANDREW LANG. Fcap. 8vo. 5s. net.
> Chicago: Way & Williams.

STREET (G. S.).
> MINIATURES AND MOODS. Fcap. 8vo. 3s. net.
> EPISODES. Post 8vo. 3s. net.
> *Transferred by the Author to the present Publisher.*
> THE AUTOBIOGRAPHY OF A BOY. (*See* MAYFAIR SET.)
> QUALES EGO; a few remarks, in particular and at large. Fcap. 8vo. 3s. 6d. net.
> New York: The Merriam Co.

SWETTENHAM (F. A.).
> MALAY SKETCHES. With Title-page and Cover Design by PATTEN WILSON. Crown 8vo. 5s. net.
> [*Second Edition.*
> New York: Macmillan & Co.

TABB (JOHN B.).
> POEMS. Sq. 32mo. 4s. 6d. net.
> Boston: Copeland & Day.

TENNYSON (FREDERICK).
> POEMS OF THE DAY AND YEAR. With a Title-page by PATTEN WILSON. Crown 8vo. 5s. net.
> Chicago: Stone & Kimball.

THIMM (CARL A.).
> A COMPLETE BIBLIOGRAPHY OF THE ART OF FENCING AND DUELLING, as practised by all European Nations from the Middle Ages to the Present Day. With a Classified Index, arranged chronologically according to Languages. Illustrated with numerous portraits of Ancient and Modern Masters of the Art. Title-pages and frontispieces of some of the earliest works.
> Portrait of the Author by WILSON STEER, and title-page designed by PATTEN WILSON. 4to. 21s. net.
> [*In preparation.*

THOMPSON (FRANCIS).
> POEMS. With Frontispiece, Title-page, and Cover Design by LAURENCE HOUSMAN. Pott 4to. 5s. net.
> [*Fourth Edition.*
> Boston: Copeland & Day.

THOMPSON (FRANCIS)—*continued.*
   SISTER SONGS: An Offering to Two Sisters. With Frontispiece, Title-page, and Cover Design by LAURENCE HOUSMAN. Pott 4to. 5s. net.
      Boston: Copeland & Day.

THOREAU (HENRY DAVID).
   POEMS OF NATURE. Selected and edited by HENRY S. SALT and FRANK B. SANBORN, with a Title-page designed by PATTEN WILSON. Fcap. 8vo. 4s. 6d. net.
      Boston and New York: Houghton, Mifflin & Co.

TRAILL (H. D.).
   FROM CAIRO TO THE SOUDAN FRONTIER. With title-page and cover designed by PATTEN WILSON. Crown 8vo. 5s. net. [*In preparation.*
      Chicago: Way & Williams.
   THE BARBAROUS BRITISHERS: A Tip-top Novel. With Title and Cover Design by AUBREY BEARDSLEY. Crown 8vo. Wrapper, 1s. net.

TYNAN HINKSON (KATHARINE).
   CUCKOO SONGS. With Title-page and Cover Design by LAURENCE HOUSMAN. Fcap. 8vo. 5s. net.
      Boston: Copeland & Day.
   MIRACLE PLAYS: OUR LORD'S COMING AND CHILDHOOD. With Six Illustrations, Title-page, and Cover Design by PATTEN WILSON. Fcap. 8vo. 4s. 6d. net.
      Chicago: Stone & Kimball.

WATSON (ROSAMUND MARRIOTT).
   VESPERTILIA AND OTHER POEMS. With a Title-page designed by R. ANNING BELL. Fcap. 8vo. 4s. 6d. net.
   A SUMMER NIGHT AND OTHER POEMS. New edition, with a decorative Title-page. Fcap. 8vo. 3s. net.
      Chicago: Way & Williams.

WATSON (WILLIAM).
   THE FATHER OF THE FOREST, AND OTHER POEMS. With New Photogravure Portrait of the Author. Fcap. 8vo. 3s. 6d. net. [*Fifth Thousand.*
      75 copies, large paper, 10s. 6d. net.
      Chicago: Stone & Kimball.
   ODES AND OTHER POEMS. Fcap. 8vo, buckram. 4s. 6d. net. [*Fourth Edition.*
      New York: Macmillan & Co.

WATSON (WILLIAM)—*continued*.
  THE ELOPING ANGELS: A Caprice. Square 16mo, buckram. 3s. 6d. net. [*Second Edition*.
  New York: Macmillan & Co.
  EXCURSIONS IN CRITICISM: being some Prose Recreations of a Rhymer. Cr. 8vo. 5s. net. [*Second Edition*.
  New York: Macmillan & Co.
  THE PRINCE'S QUEST AND OTHER POEMS. With a Bibliographical Note added. Fcap. 8vo. 4s. 6d. net.
  [*Third Edition*.
  THE PURPLE EAST: a Series of Sonnets on England's Desertion of Armenia. With a Frontispiece by G. F. WATTS, R.A. Fcap. 8vo. Wrappers, 1s. net.
  [*Third Edition*.

WATT (FRANCIS).
  THE LAW'S LUMBER ROOM. Fcap. 8vo. 3s. 6d. net.
  [*Second Edition*.
  Chicago: A. C. McClurg & Co.

WATTS (THEODORE).
  POEMS. Crown 8vo. 5s. net. [*In preparation*.
  There will also be an Edition de Luxe *of this volume printed at the Kelmscott Press.*

WHARTON (H. T.).
  SAPPHO. Memoir, Text, Selected Renderings, and a Literal Translation by HENRY THORNTON WHARTON. With three Illustrations in Photogravure, and a Cover designed by AUBREY BEARDSLEY. Fcap. 8vo. 7s. 6d. net. [*Third Edition*.
  Chicago: A. C. McClurg & Co.

THE YELLOW BOOK
An Illustrated Quarterly
Pott 4to.   5s. net.

VOLUME I. April 1894. 272 pages. 15 Illustrations.
[*Out of print*.
VOLUME II. July 1894. 364 pages. 23 Illustrations.
VOLUME III. October 1894. 280 pages. 15 Illustrations.
VOLUME IV. January 1895. 285 pages. 16 Illustrations.
VOLUME V. April 1895. 317 pages. 14 Illustrations.
VOLUME VI. July 1895. 335 pages. 16 Illustrations.
VOLUME VII. October 1895. 320 pages. 20 Illustrations.
VOLUME VIII. January 1896. 406 pages. 26 Illustrations.

www.ingramcontent.com/pod-product-compliance
Lightning Source LLC
Chambersburg PA
CBHW032132160426
43197CB00008B/616